McCarthyism
and
Consensus

THE CREDIBILITY OF INSTITUTIONS, POLICIES AND LEADERSHIP
A Series funded by the Hewlett Foundation
Kenneth W. Thompson, *Series Editor*

McCarthyism and Consensus

The Credibility of Institutions, Policies and Leadership
Volume 13

William Bragg Ewald, Jr.

Series Editor
Kenneth W. Thompson

University Press of America
Lanham • New York • London

The
White Burkett
Miller Center

Library of Congress Cataloging-in-Publication Data

Ewald, William Bragg, 1925-
  McCarthyism and consensus.

  (The Credibility of institutions, policies and
leadership ; v. 13)
  "Co-published by arrangement with the White Burkett
Miller Center of Public Affairs, University of
Virginia"—T.p. verso.
  Contents: Rotunda lecture: McCarthyism revisited /
William Bragg Ewald, Jr.—Miller Center discussion:
McCarthyism and consensus.
  1. Anti-communist movements—United States—History—
20th century. 2. McCarthy, Joseph, 1908-1957.
3. Subversive activities—United States—History—20th
century. I. White Burkett Miller Center. II. Title.
III. Series.
E743.5.E93 1986   322.4'2   86-9233
ISBN 0-8191-5433-4 (alk. paper)
ISBN 0-8191-5434-2 (pbk. : alk. paper)

The views expressed by the author(s) of this publication do not necessarily
represent the opinions of the Miller Center. We hold to Jefferson's dictum that:
"Truth is the proper and sufficient antagonist to error, and has nothing to fear
from the conflict, unless, by human interposition, disarmed of her natural
weapons, free argument and debate."

Co-published by arrangement with
The White Burkett Miller Center of Public Affairs,
University of Virginia

All University Press of America books are produced on acid-free
paper which exceeds the minimum standards set by the National
Historical Publications and Records Commission.

Contents

Preface

Kenneth W. Thompson

For a host of reasons, the American people are opposed to communism. Religious people oppose it because of its antagonistic view toward the Judaic-Christian tradition—"the opiate of the people." Labor union members are against it because Communist organizers have tried to seize control of trade unions. Corporate leaders are against communism because it aims "to bury" capitalism. For these reasons and others, the American Communist movement has never attracted the support of more than a tiny minority of the American people.

Thus there is a strong anti-Communist consensus on a general philosophical level in the United States. The debate arises over the form that consensus takes, the methods it employs and the rhetoric it uses.

McCarthyism was a movement in the 1950s which centered around the activities of the junior senator from Wisconsin. At first, there appeared to be strong support for the movement, but then a reaction set in. The role of the Eisenhower administration was important in that response, although President Eisenhower's practice of not meeting the challenge head on was much discussed and debated.

William Ewald is the author of a recent book on these issues entitled *Who Killed Joe McCarthy?* Because the Miller Center of the University of Virginia has been concerned to learn more about the several postwar presidencies, we have wanted to know more about "Eisenhower and McCarthyism." We have also been examining the problem of consensus—how it is formed, who mobilizes the consensus, what is its organizing principle and how it declines.

We are pleased that Dr. Ewald agreed to explore these issues with us. Our conference started with his lecture in the University's Rotunda. It continued the next day at the Miller Center itself, where a group of senior faculty members and community leaders met with him for an extended discussion. These two sessions, recorded, produced this book—a transcript, edited as slighty as possible, of what was said during those two days.

PART ONE

Rotunda Lecture: McCarthyism Revisited

William Bragg Ewald, Jr.

KENNETH THOMPSON: It is a great pleasure to welcome you to a lecture in the Rotunda on the subject of the Eisenhower presidency and McCarthyism. The subject of interest to the Miller Center of Public Affairs is, as you know, the study of the presidency. It would be difficult to imagine a more complex and troublesome and difficult problem with which any administration has had to deal than the problem of McCarthyism. It was a subject that those who didn't live actively in the educational or political arena at that time can hardly understand in terms of its intensity and degree of feeling. My exposure to it was very limited, and I won't belabor that tiny little experience except to say that only once in my life have I left a building with a cordon of police helping me out of the building. That was after a discussion with Senator McCarthy's campaign manager in which my subject was the limits and possibilities of collective security. It became necessary to call on the police to take us out of the building. That example shows how enormously inflammatory the issues were at that time and how deeply and passionately many felt.

Barbara Tuchman in introducing Mr. Ewald's volume writes, "The era of shame is vividly recreated for us by an insider in Eisenhower's White House who knew the participants and observed the events at close quarters. Read it and remember." Mr. Ewald has contributed to the Eisenhower portrait volume published by the Miller Center. He was, as Barbara Tuchman says, an insider in the White House, an assistant to Secretary of the Interior Fred Seaton. He served on the White House staff as a speechwriter. He wrote a biography that was widely reviewed and highly praised by the reviewers. Arthur Burns called it a literary masterpiece on the Eisenhower presidency. He collaborated with President Eisenhower on President Eisenhower's two volumes, *Mandate for Change* and *Waging Peace.*

He is currently an executive of the IBM Corporation and is well known for his skill and ability and as an evenhanded interpreter of public affairs. He was a very wise scholar in the field of literature in his own right before entering the White House, having taught in the English Department at Harvard University. We feel especially pleased that he would return to the Miller Center to discuss his new book, *Who Killed Joe McCarthy?*, an account of the struggle that went on in the Eisenhower administration in connection with the movement of McCarthyism. It is a pleasure to welcome William Bragg Ewald, Jr. to the Dome Room of the Rotunda.

MR. EWALD: Believe me, I enjoyed every word, Ken, of that very, very glowing and, I think, undeserved introduction, and I am honored and flattered by it. Let me say that as an admirer of Ken Thompson and the Miller Center and what they've been doing there, it is a real pleasure for me and for my wife Mary to come back again and have an opportunity to visit the University and to speak with you today. I'm not a Virginian, and I apologize, but I did the next best thing. I married a Virginian. My wife grew up here in the state and really loves it and feels very close to it. Many of my relatives, many friends, and all of my children are also Virginians, and so I feel I, in a sense, may be a Virginian by adoption.

Also, as Ken said, I had the honor of working for President Eisenhower. Someone once asked me whether Dwight Eisenhower had any role models, and I answered immediately that he had two role models, and they were both Virginians. One was George Washington, and one was Robert E. Lee, and there was absolutely no qualification in his admiration for both of them. He really, I've always felt, modeled himself and tried to follow the example of George Washington personally. He loved Robert E. Lee. I remember one time he was talking about painting. He liked to paint, and he said he wanted to do a portrait of Robert E. Lee, but Eisenhower was very, very modest about his painting and he said, "The only trouble was I could never get the whiskers right," and so he never finished the portrait.

It is an honor to speak here in this hallowed Jeffersonian hall on a diabolical subject. I don't know whether you saw the cover of my book, but it shows Senator McCarthy almost like a man burning in hell-flames. If you had to look at American history and find two figures who really exemplified two poles—on the one side, freedom of the mind and on the other side, obscurantism and an attempt to curtail and thwart intellectual exploration—you couldn't think of two figures who could fill those roles better than, on the one hand, Thomas Jefferson, and on the other, Joseph McCarthy.

So I would say they exemplify the root struggle in the McCarthy period, as Elmer Davis pointed out in the Phi Beta Kappa lecture at Harvard in June, 1953. It was a struggle over man's right to free inquiry and to freedom of the mind against people who wanted to thwart that in some respect. But that's not the struggle I really want to talk about here today. The struggle I've been concerned with in the book is the more immediate grainy, grimy, dirty political battle that went on day by day between a United States senator from Wisconsin elected by an overwhelming majority with a great popular following in his own state, on the one hand, and the Republican administration, an administration which shared the same political banner as McCarthy but was headed by a vastly different man, Dwight Eisenhower. That struggle, that clash is the clash that in the end destroyed McCarthy.

When I say "Who killed Joe McCarthy?" let me tell you I'm not talking about who poisoned him. I had somebody call up and say, "I know who poisoned Joe McCarthy. It's the same people who poisoned Robert Taft." That is not what I'm talking about. I'm talking about the *political* death of McCarthy, his political demise. As you probably know, he had a very, very substantial public following. He had it for many years, four and a half years, and yet at the end of that four and a half year period, at the end of the Army/McCarthy hearings, McCarthy was really a dead duck politically.

This is a controversial subject. It is controversial even to this present day as you read various reviews of the book. For example, George Will finds my argument very persuasive and he likes it, and other people don't. Barbara Tuchman also likes it, and I think this is one of the few things that George Will and Barbara

Tuchman have ever agreed on. Nonetheless, you will find a continuing controversy over this particular subject. So I say read the evidence and take your pick, and best of all read the book. Simon and Schuster, $17.95, and you can get it cheaper if you are a member of the Book-of-the-Month Club.

Now, this is not just an historical subject. At the present moment you have to look at this controversy between Eisenhower and McCarthy in a larger context—the reexamination of the Eisenhower presidency. I find that reexamination highly significant. If you listened to Governor Cuomo in his keynote speech to the Democratic convention, and if you listened to Ronald Reagan in his speech to the Republican convention, I think you noticed something rather unusual. You noticed in both parties a searching to find heroes for the party. Governor Cuomo quite obviously had his heroes, and the key hero who ran all through his speech is Franklin D. Roosevelt. He wants the Democratic party to look back to Roosevelt as hero and example and model.

President Reagan, in contrast, did a very unusual thing. He forgot the Republican heroes—forgot Nixon, forgot Herbert Hoover, forgot Calvin Coolidge, forgot Warren G. Harding. He reached over into the Democratic party and pulled the heroes he wants into the Republican party: Harry Truman, Jack Kennedy, and Hubert Humphrey. Now that is a rather neat political trick. But in both parties and particularly the Republican party there is a search for models out of the past who can guide the party in the future. And I would say that the example of Dwight Eisenhower is an example that the Republican party today ought to be taking a good look at. Eisenhower was a Republican centrist. He hated the labels "liberal" and "conservative." He said what you try to do is go down the middle and do what makes sense. Sometimes you end up doing a conservative thing, sometimes you do a liberal thing, but use the sense the good Lord gave you and go down the middle. And of course he commanded an enormous following in that center mainstream, not only of the Republican party but of the United States. He reached over into the Democratic party, and they came in droves.

The perception of Eisenhower's presidency I think will matter in the future of the Republican party. And nothing, to many people, is more central to that perception than how he dealt with

McCarthy. Did he succeed? Did he fail? Did he waffle? Was he scared to death of McCarthy? Was he a mastermind behind the scenes trying to kill off McCarthy? What was his view? How effective was he? Until we can try to come to grips with those questions I think the image of Eisenhower will continue to carry some kind of cloud over it, and people will not really understand the nature of the man and the nature of his contribution. That is really why I wrote the book, just to try to straighten out that particular feature of the Eisenhower performance. And I will say it is not a simple task. There is not a pat answer, and it is not an either/or thing. It is a difficult thing to sort out.

Let me ask for a show of hands. How many people remember Joe McCarthy and remember the era and remember having lived through it and remember watching the debates? Let's see, I guess maybe it is fifty-fifty, and a lot of people don't remember. So let me just reel off what we are talking about.

McCarthy flies out—a United States senator—on February 9, 1950 to Wheeling, West Virginia to make a routine political speech, and he gets off the plane and is met by the welcoming committee, and he says, "Gentlemen, I've got two speeches in my pocket on two different subjects written by two different staff groups. One of them is on housing and one of them is on Communists in government. Which one do you think I should give?" And the welcoming committee says, "Why don't you do the one on Communists and government? That has a little more sex appeal." So McCarthy says okay. He gets up that night and pulls out of his pocket a speech in which he claims, "I have here in my hand a list of 205 members of the Communist party who today are in high offices in the State Department making U.S. policy, and they are known to Secretary of State Dean Acheson."

From there on McCarthy is on page one. He is a leader in the anti-Communist movement. People follow him. They want to find out what he knows, what spies he can identify and so on. He goes on from there in the course of the following months and calls General George C. Marshall—the United States Army Chief of Staff during World War II—calls him a man who has served the Communist conspiracy, a traitor to the country. He goes after the State Department. He investigates the Voice of America and investigates a lot of people. In the end he investigates the United States Army, not the people in uniform but the civilians in the Department of the Army. And he is onto something. He thinks there are a lot of Communists in one of their installations, and he is carrying forward this investigation. Meanwhile, on his staff he has a young man named G. David Schine. G. David Schine has registered for the draft, and his draft board acts, puts him in 1A and says you are going into the Army, and they put him in the Army. So these two things are going along concurrently—McCarthy's investigation and Schine's being drafted into the Army—and they lead to the confrontation, a series of charges and countercharges. The Army charges that McCarthy is seeking special favors in the Army for Private Schine, trying to get him out of K.P. on Sunday, to give him weekends and evenings off. That kind of thing. That's one charge—that McCarthy's abusing his power, McCarthy and his chief counsel, Roy Cohn.

On the other side McCarthy comes back with his countercharge against the Army. He says, "Look, you've got this young man in the Army as a private, and you are using him as a hostage. You are twisting my arm. You are trying to make life tough for him to get me to cut off my investigation of the Army."

They make all these charges and countercharges public. The Senate committee has to investigate them, and between April 1954 and June 1954 the Army-McCarthy hearings air all these grievances and accusations. Those hearings, by the time they were over, killed McCarthy.

I walked into the White House at eight o'clock in the morning on July 26, 1954, about a month and a half after the hearings had ended, and from that date on I can tell you we didn't spend one minute or one hour or one day worrying about Joe McCarthy or about what he thought or about what his influence was, or about his political power. He was dead, dead, dead, and I remind you that in those months we were going through a congressional election in which he had promised the issue of Communists in government would be the key issue. People didn't want him to speak for them. He was out of it and remained out of it, and he walked around like one of the living dead for several more years and finally died in 1957.

In December of 1954, to be sure, the United States Senate

voted a censure motion against McCarthy, a very rare action by the Senate, and that put the final nail in his coffin. But believe me, they would not have voted that censure action had he not been politically prostrate at the end of the Army/McCarthy hearings.

As you can imagine, there have been millions of words written about this, and many books. Why do another one? What I was trying to do was really to straighten out and fill out the factual record and to answer the question: What was it exactly that brought McCarthy down, that really destroyed him? Because to this time I had never seen a really satisfactory answer. People just have the idea that the American people got tired of him or he just kind of came to an end. During McCarthy's life he sowed confusion, hysteria, distortion, misunderstanding, and misinformation, and to this day that question is still clouded with these same things.

Now it is great to say you want to get new information and want to add to the record. How do you do so when the record has been done to death? Well, to quote McCarthy himself, let me say I have here in my hand a three-page transcript, single-spaced, of a telephone call. I've got reams of these. This one was a phone call between the Secretary of the Army, Robert Stevens, and Struve Hensel, the general counsel for the Department of Defense, and they are discussing what they ought to be doing about McCarthy.

This cache of records, of new documents, was locked up during the Army/McCarthy hearings by order of President Eisenhower. They were documents of various sorts. They were memoranda and records of conferences, they were day-by-day chronologies, and above all they were these memoranda of telephone conversations. The Secretary of the Army and other people in the Pentagon didn't tape conversations the way Nixon did or the way Charles Wick did or other people have; they didn't have modern technology. Instead, the Secretary of the Army had a guy sitting outside his office around the corner at a little desk with a phone cradled on his shoulder, and when the Secretary takes an incoming call, this aide also picks up the phone and listens in without telling the incoming caller. And he is a very fast shorthand operator, and he takes it all down and fills little spiral books with it.

These conversations in the Pentagon went on and on and on for months and months. At the climax of the hearings the verbatim transcripts were locked up. They never saw the light of day. McCarthy would have loved to have got his hands on them. He never did. They remained in the possession of the executive branch and have there remained until this book came out, and there they are for the first time published. They are now public documents. And the value of those documents is to permit someone for the first time to reconstruct a narrative that goes along day by day, minute by minute through this whole period of months where you have these controversies going on, and you can see who is doing what and who is taking what action and how people were responding to one another. So that is one source of new information.

The second source was interviews with people who really were behind the closed doors where they were figuring out what to do about McCarthy. Sherman Adams, Eisenhower's chief of staff, was one of them. Jim Hagerty, Eisenhower's press secretary, was another. I interviewed Jim before he died. I have access to Jim's diary and I've used that. Ken Thompson mentioned that I worked for Fred Seaton when Fred was in the Department of the Interior. I had known him when we were both on the White House staff. During the McCarthy battle Fred was the White House man in the Pentagon, *the* agent of Eisenhower and Adams: believe me, there were no other agents. He was the man who gathered all these papers together and took them with him, kept them with him all through his time in Washington and at the end of his career in Washington took them with him to his home out in Hastings, Nebraska where they remained until his death.

Joe Welch, who was the Army special counsel, died soon after the hearings. But his number two man, Jim St. Clair, couldn't have been more helpful in recalling things that they did and trying to straighten out the record. All these major figures— Struve Hensel was another one—on the administration side who are today alive I've talked to and have had wholehearted recollection and help from, and I've talked with a lot of minor characters, like the man who actually picked up these papers and carried them across the Potomac from the Pentagon to the White House. Or like the man who carried around the briefcase for Joe

Welch and followed him like a shadow, night and day, through the whole of the hearings. Nobody even knows who he was. Anyway, he talked to me at great length. So I like to think that the result is a book that, in my view, reads like a novel and goes behind the scenes. The upshot of the book is, I believe, that it disproves the easy, simple, pat myths about who killed Joe McCarthy, such as the myth that McCarthy was killed by booze. Now, there's no question that McCarthy drank like a fish. Witnesses recall he would drink in the morning, he'd drink before breakfast, he'd drink after breakfast, he'd drink before he went to work, he would drink at lunch, he'd drink in the afternoon, he'd drink in the evening and he sometimes would drink all night with drinking buddies who slept, I guess, during the day while he was working. He was a heavy drinker. But booze, to my mind, had nothing whatsoever to do with his political demise. If he had never touched a drop, I think the story of McCarthy and McCarthyism would have turned out much the same.

The second answer to who killed Joe McCarthy politically is often Roy Cohn. You have probably heard this. Here is this sharp young lawyer leading this bumbling, noisy senator around by the nose and getting him into a lot of trouble. You talk to friends of McCarthy today, and some of them don't like Roy Cohn. Roy Cohn himself still admires McCarthy. But though some people have tried to put the blame on Roy, I don't believe he killed Joe McCarthy, and I do not see Roy Cohn as the problem either. Joe McCarthy was the problem.

Some of you may remember Edward R. Murrow's famous telecast against McCarthy on "See It Now," in prime time early in 1954. A lot of people say Edward R. Murrow killed McCarthy with that single telecast. Other people say it was Herblock of the *Washington Post* who killed him with his cartoons. I don't believe either, although Murrow had a part in it, and Herblock hacked away at McCarthy day after day, but basically they were adjuncts to something more central.

Army Counsel Joe Welch, a Boston lawyer, pixieish, gentle, dapper, shrewd, with an instinct for the jugular—there is no doubt during the hearings that he became a folk figure beloved by millions of Americans watching television, and people will tell you today that Joe Welch, after everybody else had failed, came to

Washington and killed McCarthy. I don't believe that either. Joe Welch came in very late, he did a very special job, and it was a very crucial job in the destruction of McCarthy. But he didn't do it all by himself singlehandedly. I'll give you one fact. In the month before Joe Welch came to Washington, McCarthy's public opinion rating dropped from forty-six percent approval to thirty-eight percent approval—for the first time a significant downward drop. Joe Welch hadn't even been selected then.

A beautiful and chic and knowledgeable friend of ours once said, "I know who killed Joe McCarthy. It was Bob and Ray." That's one I had never heard before. She said they killed him by making fun of him. Well, I don't think Bob and Ray killed him either.

Now, I've left out one name, Dwight Eisenhower. What role did he have? There are two simple pat explanations of the Eisenhower role. (A) Eisenhower didn't do anything. He was scared to death of McCarthy. He tried to stay away from him. He didn't want to get involved. He let other people take the heat. He let other people suffer. He got as far away as he could. That's one answer. And it's wrong. (B) The second answer—a more recent answer that started to appear as people looked at the Eisenhower role and looked at some of the evidence—swings all the way over to the other side. This answer is that Dwight Eisenhower singlehandedly brought McCarthy down, brought him down by maneuvering behind the scenes, pulling strings. He knew everything that went on, this answer goes, day by day. He sat there in the Oval Office, worked through his agents, pulled these wires, controlled everything, and with a singleminded purpose brought McCarthy down all by himself. This answer exemplifies the conception of Eisenhower the sneak—the man so clever and diabolical and Machiavellian that he could kill people and still seem to rise above it all with his nice grin and seem not to be hurting anybody. I find that explanation wrong also. And I'll tell you one reason why.

If you look at that spring in 1954, Eisenhower wasn't sitting there in the White House worrying about McCarthy all the time. In fact, I don't think Eisenhower worried about McCarthy even as much as fifty percent of his time or forty percent. You know what he was worrying about in the spring of 1954? Among other things he was worrying about whether we should go into

Vietnam. Believe me, that was a far more agonizing decision, a far more intricate decision. He had to worry with the French, the British, the Vietnamese, and the American people trying to sort his way out through that whole business.

The spring of 1954 was also the spring when the Supreme Court announced its Brown vs. Board of Education decision on school integration. It was also a time in which Eisenhower spent many, many weeks on something people have now forgotten called the Bricker Amendment, which would have curtailed the power of the President to make treaties. He had a lot on his plate, including the biggest legislative program he ever introduced to the Congress. So to say that he was sitting there worrying exclusively about McCarthy, I find an exaggeration.

Therefore, what I've tried to do is tell the story, lay out the history. It's almost like asking what happened in *War and Peace* and having somebody come back at you and say, "Look, you don't have to read that book. I'll tell you. Napoleon lost." Sure, McCarthy was defeated. But the exciting part is the action on the battlefield. It reminds you of some of the scenes in *Henry IV, Part One* or *Henry V* where you see a skirmish over here, and then the scene changes and you get a skirmish over there, and people are engaged in conflict in the middle of the night. They don't know what the other people are doing on the battlefield. It's that kind of a rolling action that you have all through these months. It is absolutely absorbing, and in the end it results in McCarthy's death. In that action Dwight Eisenhower is a central figure, no question about it. But, believe me, he didn't do everything perfectly. He made a lot of mistakes. There were a lot of things he didn't know about and a lot of things he didn't control, and there was a lot of sheer dumb luck in the whole episode.

That's where I find reconstructing history far more fascinating than spinning theories. And that's what I've tried to do. In this history you have a great cast of characters. New York Governor Thomas E. Dewey, for example, who ran against Truman in 1948 and was a big Eisenhower backer. Most people don't even know he had a part in this whole thing. Well, he did have a part, way behind the scenes. He was the man who really, as much as anybody, helped pick Joe Welch and put him in there. Nobody knew that at the time.

Secondly, you have Morris Ernst, the great civil libertarian, the lawyer who successfully defended the sending through the mail of James Joyce's *Ulysses* in the early 1930's. Morris Ernst had a part in this, and it is a very fascinating part because Morris Ernst managed to penetrate the McCarthy organization and was supplying information to the Army's side. Nobody knew about that. There are dozens of other people who had actions in this fight. I had a very nice letter, as a matter of fact, a couple of days ago from Senator Stuart Symington, who was a Democrat on the McCarthy committee and a political opponent to the Republicans. He said he had read the book and admired it very much and liked it, and I thought that was a very gracious thing for him to say because obviously there were some political tensions in there. McCarthy was very rough on Symington, and the Administration to a certain extent was also rough on Symington. He's a gentleman.

So what I've tried to do is establish a piece of history. I believe you get a great overriding lesson out of the book that we ought to remember and that is this: what do you do about a demagogue, about a man who is standing up and exaggerating or distorting or falsifying for some kind of political purpose and who has a following? How do you get rid of him? We've had demagogues. We're going to have demagogues for as long as you can imagine. We've had them from the time of Alcibiades. He's in Thucydides. He's in Plutarch. We've had Hitler in our own time. We've had Huey Long. And we've had McCarthy. We've had a lot of them, and we're going to have more. It seems to me that it is not a bad idea to look at some case studies. There are certain ways in which you cannot bring down a demagogue. I'd say that the main thing that you need is what Thomas Jefferson said we needed, eternal vigilance. People have to have their eyes open. They have to be aware. They have to be paying attention. They have to be adding up: if a man says two plus two equals five, they have to do their addition themselves and cut him off. That's one thing. Without that you can't do anything.

The other thing that you need is something that you get by looking, as this book does, at the Eisenhower conduct. You need some very hardheaded, practical, realistic sense about what options are open to you. People will say, why didn't Eisenhower within five minutes get rid of McCarthy? One woman wrote to the President and said, "Mr. President, I think you ought to fire

McCarthy." Well, no president can fire a senator. It is hard enough to get a censure vote. The people of Wisconsin could have voted for McCarthy's opponent, but they didn't. Well then, the argument goes. Eisenhower should have got up and delivered a speech that instantaneously would have floored McCarthy. Well, Eisenhower had around him excellent speechwriters. He had denunciatory speech drafts handed to him by people as red in the face about McCarthy as they could get. They were furious. They thought a speech would do it.

Eisenhower, in fact, got exactly this advice from the most trusted of all his advisors—a man whose judgment, integrity, honesty, and sense he admired certainly as much as anybody else's and possibly more: his brother Milton. Look at Milton Eisenhower's career. Milton had been a government civil servant in the Agriculture Department, in the State Department. He'd worked for President Roosevelt on special missions during the war. He served in the OWI with Elmer Davis. For heaven's sakes, Milton Eisenhower was the kind of guy McCarthy would have loved to hate, and in fact, McCarthy denounced Milton Eisenhower in a public broadcast in Wisconsin as a nefarious influence on the administration. Milton would sit there in the Oval Office with his brother Ike and he'd say, "Ike, look, you've got to make this speech. You've got to tear him apart." Dwight Eisenhower wasn't playing games with Milton. He would say, "That's not the way to do it. It will only backfire. It will only build him up, make him bigger, add to his power and into the bargain probably draw down upon me as President the fury of the entire United States Senate because let me tell you, it's a club. No President goes around attacking one member of the Senate without having the rest of them coalesce behind him." And they *would* have coalesced behind an injured member. So I ask, given those limitations, what do you do? How do you bring him down? That's what the problem was, and the book tells how it was done.

QUESTION: Could you describe that strategy in a little more detail, the Eisenhower strategy? I can read the book, I know, but just give me a preview.

MR. EWALD: I would say that Eisenhower's strategy basically boiled down to three things. He wrote in his diary April 1, 1953 that the best way in the end to deal with a demagogue of the McCarthy type was not to get into the headlines with him, to counterpunch. Now Harry S. Truman made that mistake: he counterpunched against McCarthy. Dean Acheson counterpunched against McCarthy. And the counterpunching went on for three long years before Eisenhower ever entered the office, and at the end of those three years McCarthy was bigger than ever. He could make any kind of an outlandish allegation and the White House or somebody else would respond, and you would have two columns, "McCarthy says this" and "The President says that," and you had that battle going on. Eisenhower recognized that this was page one stuff. It was the kind of thing reporters couldn't resist, and therefore he wasn't going to contribute to it personally. I mentioned the fact that he did not want to take on the United States Senate. He knew what would happen if he got into this kind of counterpunching. It is an institutional reaction with the Senate. That's number one.

The second thing was that Eisenhower had a funny way of dealing with his organization. He had people whom he trusted absolutely implicitly. He would give them a great deal of latitude and freedom to go out and to improvise and do things without his immediate control and command. He had a big organization. It was a divided organization. The White House staff was split down the middle—some people for appeasing McCarthy, some people for socking McCarthy. The same thing was true with senators up on the Hill in the Republican party and with the Republican National Committee. You had a great division in the party. But what actually happened as this whole thing unfolded was that you got a nucleus of four men, you could call them the gang of four, who were Eisenhower followers determined to deal with the McCarthy problem and who fundamentally were hostile to McCarthy. Among them was Sherman Adams, Eisenhower's chief of staff. Sherman Adams could make a decision in Eisenhower's name. Believe me, Eisenhower may have spent a lot of time on all those other problems, but Adams spent a lot of time on McCarthy. The second one was Jim Hagerty, Eisenhower's press secretary. If you look at the Hagerty diaries you see the conversations Hagerty had with the President, that Hagerty had with Adams and with other people. He was a man in the White House who was part of this organization.

Now, across the river in the Pentagon you had two men who were totally trusted by the White House: two men and only two men. One of them was Struve Hensel, general counsel for the Department of Defense. Struve Hensel was the man who really took the Army's charges against McCarthy and polished them and got them into shape and masterminded their basic strategy.

The fourth man and in some respects the most important man of the four was Fred Seaton, whom I've mentioned. Fred had the job of being the Assistant Secretary of Defense for Legislative Affairs; he had responsibility for keeping the Congress happy. That was half his job. The other half was to keep the press happy. He was the press relations man. Fred, in that role, spent as much time in the White House as he did in the Pentagon, but he went back and forth like a shuttlecock between the two places and helped work out strategy. He and Adams and Hensel and Hagerty in effect became the agents of the President to work through the practical problems. That's part number two.

The third part is that Eisenhower constantly tried to assert principles that he believed in and which he believed the American people ought to rally around. People say he never attacked McCarthy. Well, he never attacked McCarthy by name, but if you could read and you knew how to spell and you knew how to watch television, you knew what he thought.

Those I think are the three things. And at the end of the hearings the American people saw that you've got the decent people on one side, and you've got the skulduggery on the other. You've got the decent anti-Communists over here on one side, against McCarthy. And who were they? They were Richard Nixon, who finally jumped and became an anti-McCarthyite: you couldn't call him a Communist; Herbert Brownell, Attorney General of the United States, the deviser of the Eisenhower internal security program, a man who made the speech revealing Harry Dexter White as a Communist spy in the Truman administration: Brownell was no Communist; and behind him Bill Rogers, who had been doing anti-Communist things on the Hill before McCarthy ever heard of them. And finally, last but not least, guess who was on Eisenhower's side. J. Edgar Hoover. No question about it. In the hearings the time came when he had to jump. And he jumped against McCarthy and for Eisenhower. So what are you going to do if you are an American citizen and you are a good anti-Communist? You line up. You have a choice. You can either go with Ike and Nixon and Brownell and Hoover; or you can go with Joe. And the American people in the end said to hell with it. They went with Eisenhower.

QUESTION: Did the FBI feed information to Joe McCarthy?

MR. EWALD: If you read the book, you'll find out. The allegation that the FBI did is a good example of historical inference: I don't like Joe McCarthy; I don't like J. Edgar Hoover; therefore Hoover was feeding data to McCarthy. Hoover went sour in the 1960's, without question. Arthur Schlesinger said, "There is only one man who says McCarthy didn't get anything from J. Edgar Hoover. Guess who he is: Roy Cohn." So Arthur M. Schlesinger goes right down the line accusing Hoover on dubious second-hand evidence. He had no solid proof whatsoever that Hoover was feeding stuff to McCarthy after Eisenhower came in. I have to qualify that. He may have fed him stuff during the Truman administration. That I don't know, but not after Eisenhower came in.

I thought there was only one way to answer that question. So I went to the FBI under the Freedom of Information Act and said: Give me the documents that tell what J. Edgar Hoover was doing, what relationship he had with the McCarthy subcommittee. And they came back with documents, some of them typed, some of them in the scrawled handwriting of J. Edgar Hoover, and I'll tell you what they boiled down to. What would you do if you were J. Edgar Hoover, head of the FBI, Mr. Anti-Communist-subversion, your appropriations depending upon your primacy in this field and on the effectiveness of your networks and your agents? Would you throw your best secrets up to this crazy nut on the Hill? You wouldn't, and he didn't. J. Edgar Hoover saw McCarthy, from the Bureau's point of view, as nothing but trouble, trouble, trouble. Sure, he played around with McCarthy a lot. He would go to the racetrack with him, they would have dinner together, they were pals. But underneath he didn't give him a thing and that fact is documented in any number of internal memoranda written by Hoover and his top aides Clyde Tolson and Louis Nichols. They were very, very firm on that.

Hoover hated the idea that McCarthy would hire ex-FBI agents for his staff. If he hires enough of these guys, Hoover said, they'll be on the phone calling our people, and pretty soon our own network will unravel.

QUESTION: In your view, did television not play a significant role in the confrontation between Senator McCarthy and Attorney Welch?

MR EWALD: That confrontation I believe climaxed the whole drama. And when I said that Joe Welch didn't kill McCarthy, I meant that Joe Welch didn't kill him singlehandedly, with nothing having happened until Welch arrived on the scene. Welch was a very significant figure, and through the hearings, as I pointed out, you had Welch's very brilliant exploitation of a group of accidents that just happened out of the blue and that in the end had the effect of making McCarthy look worse and less decent and less reliable in the eyes of the huge television-watching public. They saw McCarthy contrasted with Welch, and there is no question that that contrast played a central part in the whole result. The climactic moment in the destruction of McCarthy came when McCarthy attacked a young lawyer in Welch's law firm for having had Communist associations a number of years before, and Welch at that moment got up and went for the jugular. People have never forgotten that moment. But it was a part of a big mosaic, a wonderful dramatic part.

QUESTION: A reviewer in yesterday's *New York Times* didn't exactly buy your thesis, and I wonder how you answered his question which was if Eisenhower was masterminding this attack on McCarthy, why did he approve of the firing of 1,400 government employees?

MR. EWALD: Well, he didn't quite say that. What that particular reviewer did was to claim that I said that Eisenhower did everything flawlessly. Well, if you read the book, you'll see that's the first disclaimer I make. Eisenhower didn't do things flawlessly. Then the reviewer said, "Well, the fact that Sherman Adams and Jim Hagerty and Fred Seaton and Struve Hensel were working against McCarthy doesn't prove Eisenhower was against him. Maybe they did it all on their own." For that conclusion he's got not a shred of evidence. Those four men were working for Ike, and Ike knew what they were doing. He would look in on them from time to time. And believe me, if he didn't like what they were doing he would have called in Sherman Adams and said, "Sherm, cease and desist," and Adams would have done it. They were agents of Eisenhower, no question about it.

That reviewer seems to believe he discovered a fact I'd missed: that the United States was worried about Communism. Well, I tried until I was blue in the face—I'll show you the passage if you want—to say the whole McCarthy movement began with a great public concern over the possibility of domestic subversion in the government. Both Eisenhower and Stevenson campaigned in 1952 on a platform that we're going to go down to Washington and straighten things out. Stevenson had to do it a little bit more gingerly because he was Harry Truman's boy and Harry Truman was the incumbent. But Eisenhower made no bones about it: The faith of the American people in the integrity and loyalty of the government has been undermined, and that is shaking the country up. Until we can get in there and clean up the mess and get the answers in an honest fashion, the country is going to continue to be all shook up.

So Ike set up a security program to get rid of security risks— not just Communists but people who were drunks, who had a criminal record or who had personal problems that could make them security risks. Eisenhower said we have to come in after twenty years of Roosevelt and Truman and the New Deal and Fair Deal, and the new broom is going to sweep clean, and it did. Attorney General Brownell devised the security program. Brownell is a civil libertarian as much as anybody. He is like Earl Warren. And if you will read an article written by Anthony Lewis in July of 1956 explaining what had been happening in Washington under Eisenhower, Lewis said his tough security risk program had restored the faith of the American people in their government. That is Anthony Lewis—no McCarthyite.

Eisenhower and Brownell recognized they had a problem. They solved the problem. McCarthy was only making that problem worse. He was just a rogue elephant, and they wanted to cut themselves loose from him and they did. That's a long answer to one allegation.

QUESTION: McCarthy always had that list or paper that he waved before the public. Was there a list of names?

MR. EWALD: No. He had no list of names in his hand or anywhere else. The story of the Wheeling speech would be funny if it weren't so sad. He went out there, and he really didn't think he was going to do much of anything in speaking at Wheeling. He didn't think he was going to make any waves—say anything anybody would remember. So he made that wild claim. Then from Wheeling he went on to Salt Lake City. When he gets to Denver, the plane has to stop for more fuel, and he gets off and a bunch of reporters descend on him. They say, "Joe, where is that list? Where are the names?" So he thinks fast and he says, " Well, fellows, I've got the names and I've got the list, but unfortunately they are still on the plane. They are in another suit that is in my luggage. But I'll tell you what you do. You send a wire or make a phone call to Dean Acheson and tell him that if he'll call me when I get to Salt Lake City, I'll give him the names." Well, that was a play for the headlines all right. He knew perfectly well the Secretary of State wasn't going to pick up the phone and say, "Joe, give me the names."

Somebody took a tape of his original speech and played it over a Wheeling, West Virginia radio, and after they finished they said, "Well, that's all we'll ever need of that speech, and we might as well use the tape for something else." So they recorded over it. And no real record exists of what McCarthy actually uttered. But his 205 figure was in his original script, though he changed the number later. But he had no list of names high up in the current State Department. He did come up with names of people, familiar names, later on trying to answer his critics, but that original accusation was a barefaced lie.

MR. THOMPSON: You have some idea why a visitor and friend said when Bill Ewald left the teaching of English that it was the discipline's great loss. He would have been and still can be a great teacher, and he has shown that. It has been a great pleasure to have you speak.

PART TWO

Miller Center Discussion: McCarthyism and Consensus

KENNETH THOMPSON: I am delighted to welcome all of you to the Miller Center.

We are glad that we can continue here the discussion that started yesterday in the Dome Room of the Rotunda. There some of you may have heard Bill Ewald make a presentation on the substance of his book. That same subject certainly is the central theme of our discussion this morning. However, we also are extremely interested at the Miller Center in the question of consensus. To what extent, we have asked ourselves, did McCarthyism represent an underlying consensus on anti-communism in this country, a consensus which propelled someone into a position of considerable power and authority who in the absence of that consensus surely would have had difficulty doing some of the things that he did? The consensus was strong enough so that practices were followed in universities and colleges that at least in my lifetime have never been followed in quite that way.

For instance, when I was a young assistant professor at Northwestern University, two of McCarthy's strongest supporters, Kenneth Colegrove and William Tecumseh McGovern, were faculty members there. McGovern wrote introductions to several of McCarthy's books of speeches.

Kenneth Colegrove, who was a gracious and charming man and who was the first when a child was born or someone was to be married to send greetings and give gifts, nevertheless felt so strongly on the clear and present danger or threat that he assigned two or three graduate students to come to each assistant professor's classes to take notes and deliver the notes to him following the classes. This went on through the semester. I think if he were here, Kenneth would say that it was vital to determine what young professors were telling the students because of the strong danger created by this Communist threat.

That attitude is one reason it seemed to us that a question worth posing was how much consensus was there on this type of anti-communism? And, secondly, how much consensus did President Eisenhower think there was on anti-communism in the country? To what extent was this a factor he had to take into account? I think Bill Ewald doesn't assess that as directly as he does certain other issues, but there are references in his book that refer to the five hundred thousand to two hundred thousand victory of McCarthy in Wisconsin and to other statistics of this kind and the forty-six to thirty-eight percent favorable view of McCarthy which gets reversed as the country reacts against his tactics. Was this something which had fairly deep roots of support? Was there a consensus on McCarthyism? Was it a "near miss?"

And the third issue which is brought into the consensus that interests us at the Miller Center is how does a President deal with an issue of this kind? It is an issue involving an elected senator in the most prestigious body of the Congress, an issue which involves the continued support of a major political party in its governance and an issue which involves division within the ranks of that party and within those who govern the party.

In any case, for these and many other reasons it seemed to us it would be terribly helpful to have a smaller group discuss these issues with Bill Ewald. It seems appropriate that Bill kick off the discussion as he sees fit. Maybe you have read his book. Some of you may want to read it if you haven't already done so.

MR. EWALD: Thanks very much. As I said yesterday I am an admirer of Ken Thompson and of the Miller Center. A couple of years ago I participated here in a discussion on the Eisenhower presidency, and that volume has just come out, and I've told Ken I thought it was a smashingly good volume with a wonderful array of interviews and very useful insights. So Mary and I are delighted to come back.

When Ken was mentioning taking notes on what people were teaching I couldn't help thinking this is an ancient art. Mary used to teach nineteenth century English literature, and she came across a wonderful story about Wordsworth and Coleridge, who at one time in their checkered career were both considered subversives of some sort. You can't imagine two less dangerous subversives than William Wordsworth and Coleridge, but at any rate some kind of gumshoe was sent out to spy on them and report back what they were talking about. They were at the seaside, weren't they, Mary? At any rate he stood back in the bushes and listened, and then went back and reported he was sure they were spies because they kept talking about somebody called Spy Noza.

Maybe that is a little illustration of what can happen to a problem when it gets into the hands of the incompetent or the opportunistic. I think a strong national consensus did exist on the subject of domestic anti-communism. I think it was a consensus that built up over the postwar years. You can go back to 1945 when Ambassador Patrick Hurley came back from China and announced that we were going to lose China because you had some subversives in the State Department who were undermining American Far Eastern policy.

Pat Hurley, a flamboyant character, actually announced his resignation as ambassador at a speech at the National Press Club which Harry Truman heard about from the press. Hurley for a while was kind of a joke—a noisy Oklahoman, a rough and tough man from the Wild West coming back accusing our State Department of being Communistic.

In 1947 you had the beginning of the hearings of the House Un-American Activities Committee under the renowned J. Parnell Thomas, a Republican from New Jersey who went after the Hollywood Ten. That committee got a lot of criticism, and the Hollywood Ten had a lot of people supporting them.

Then you had Elizabeth Bentley in the fall of 1948 coming in before the House and Senate committees making accusations higher up. She said she knew red agents in the Roosevelt White House and in the Treasury Department. She named Harry Dexter White of Treasury, and William Remington in the

Commerce Department. Well, again, the question was: is she a liar? She's a self confessed former Communist spy herself. Can you trust her?

Then came the big watershed case, the Alger Hiss-Whittaker Chambers episode. When Whittaker Chambers got up before the House Un-American Activities Committee in the fall of 1948, everybody thought he was a joke. Here was this no-good pudgy character coming out on the national scene and accusing Alger Hiss. Hiss had all the tickets. He had had a distinguished college career; he'd been a clerk to Oliver Wendell Holmes; he was head of the Carnegie Endowment. He was Mr. Clean, and everybody thought that this was really just witch-hunting.

Then two major events took place that really changed people's opinion. On the 21st of January 1950 Alger Hiss was finally convicted. When you get a conviction, it is pretty hard just to walk away and say Whittaker Chambers is a joke. You have to scratch your head and wonder whether or not maybe, just maybe, there might be something in what he is saying. Then a few weeks later out of England comes the revelation that Dr. Klaus Fuchs, a very renowned atomic physicist who had worked on the atomic bomb during World War II, was a Soviet spy.

Six days after the Fuchs revelation McCarthy flies out to Wheeling, West Virginia and makes his speech claiming he had here in his hand a list of two hundred and five Communists high up in the State Department. He had crossed a divide—a divide between suspicion and the naming of names. Up to that time, Richard Nixon, Karl Mundt, and others had claimed the State Department looked suspicious in the extreme. But McCarthy said, "I can tell you who they are."

That assertion was a lie. But in the circumstances of the moment, given the American people's questioning and doubt about the extent of penetration of the American government by Soviet agents, they would listen to him, even when McCarthy failed to produce the names, even when he changed the numbers. He was leading the charge. He was going to solve a national problem.

So basically what you have is a liar exploiting a genuine national concern. This concern lasted all the way to June 1954, four and a half years later, when after the Army/McCarthy hearings, a public opinion poll showed only seven percent actually believed no Communists remained in the government.

Concern about penetration of the government—I think that is really where you have to start. Who shared this concern? Eisenhower shared it. In the 1952 campaign the whole Republican party shared it. It was an obvious black mark on the record of Harry Truman and Dean Acheson, who inadvertently got themselves boxed into a corner, in a political knee-jerk reaction.

Remember the Alger Hiss case. When they brought Truman the news he told a press conference, "This is a red herring." Somebody put the words into his mouth, but nonetheless that's what it came down to. It's a red herring, Truman said, brought out by this no-good Republican do-nothing Congress to distract public attention.

According to another story somebody privately brought Truman records about Hiss and he looked at the records and said something quite different: "Why the S.O.B., he betrayed his country." Dean Acheson also boxed himself in: "I will not turn my back on Alger Hiss." By appearing publicly to side with Hiss, Truman and Acheson handed the Republicans an issue for the 1952 campaign.

That year even Adlai Stevenson had to pledge that he was going to go to Washington and clean up the mess. He was going to do it in his way and not McCarthy's, and he made that very clear. But he did not deny the existence of a problem. I don't think anybody really denied the existence of a problem of some sort. I don't mean the problem of the presence of genuine Communists in the State Department who were actually subverting the government. I don't think that has ever been proved. The problem was: given the evidence, is this something worth looking into? Is it something that we don't really understand and that could possibly present a danger? That I think is the consensus—what people agreed on and continued to agree on for a long time.

So you have to look at the performance of Eisenhower and all these others in the light of that consensus. Eisenhower wanted to restore the confidence of the country in the government, to remove that overhanging question about the possibility of subversion. Until you removed it, the government was going to be shaken up, McCarthy was going to ride high, and people were going to allow this problem to consume all their attention, he thought.

MR.THOMPSON: That's a good stopping point. As you know, the book goes on from this point to describe in depth Eisenhower's handling of it. But it is a good point in terms of the Miller Center to ask what some of you think about this picture and the attitudes of the American people then.

QUESTION: I think it can be dangerous to regard consensus as if its shape were predetermined. It may be the function of a leader to sort of direct consensus and give it character. I'd like to hear you evaluate Ike's performance as leader, especially given the nasty character that McCarthyism took and the anti-civil libertarian direction that McCarthyism in the absence of resistance took.

MR. EWALD: I think you have to clear the board. Eisenhower loathed McCarthy personally. He had a particularly personal reason for loathing him—McCarthy's attack on George Marshall. One of the first questions he was asked, in August 1952, even before he started campaigning, was: what do you think of these McCarthy charges? This was in a press conference out in Denver. Ike stood up from behind his desk, he got red-faced, he pounded the table and walked around and said, "I'm not going to talk about individuals. I'm not going to attack an individual senator, but I'll tell you this: George Marshall was the finest kind of patriot I've ever known." He gave a glowing tribute to Marshall and he said, "If I could say anything more laudatory about Marshall, I would say it. But there was nothing, absolutely no disloyalty whatsoever, in George Marshall's soul." He went on at great length.

I'm sure you recall the episode in Wisconsin when he was going to put a paragraph into his Milwaukee speech praising Marshall and was talked out of it, for political reasons. He wanted to say this kind of thing right on McCarthy's home turf, and all his most powerful political advisers to a man said you can't go into Wisconsin with a United States senator running for office sitting there on the platform, and punch him in the nose. It'll kill you in Wisconsin. It'll kill the Republican party. It is going to hurt your good friend the Republican governor who is running and who has worked his heart out for you to get you the nomination. Governor Kohler of Wisconsin had indeed been a moving force. He begged Eisenhower to take that paragraph out. So Ike took it out. It was a terrible mistake. He never got over it. He was defensive about it.

So from the start Eisenhower had no use for McCarthy. Incidentally, before he went into Wisconsin he told McCarthy so. They had a private confrontation in Eisenhower's hotel room in Peoria, and he blistered McCarthy mercilessly.

The question is: what do you do, and what options do you have? Eisenhower made up his mind very early that he was not going to attack McCarthy by name. You say that was a mistake. But Eisenhower had a funny thing about attacking people by name. You wouldn't say he was pro-Russian, but he never attacked Joe Stalin by name. There were people who wanted him to. In his first State of the Union message, someone brought him a sentence taking a swing at Stalin. Ike struck that out and said, "I'm not going to attack Stalin personally. I may have to negotiate with him some day." He didn't want to turn national differences into a personal confrontation. The same with McCarthy. He though Harry Truman made a big mistake in answering McCarthy with punch and counterpunch—absolutely the wrong way to bring a man like that down.

Now a lot of people think Eisenhower was taking the easy way out—taking a stand on high principle to cover up the fact that he was scared, chicken-livered, afraid of McCarthy.

All I can say is that the evidence I have for Ike's strategy is something he wrote down in his secret diary on April 1, 1953: "I think the most effective strategy is to ignore him." That was not written for public consumption. That was for himself.

Next, Eisenhower repeatedly upheld certain courses of action that he wanted to get the American people to follow. He went up to Dartmouth and made an off-the-cuff speech saying don't join the bookburners. When he talked about bookburners, nobody in the United States of America could fail to know whom he was talking about. It was McCarthy. It was also Cohn and Schine, who had just made their whirlwind tour around Europe trying to find subversive books in U. S. overseas libraries.

A few weeks later McCarthy hired a man as his staff director who had written an article attacking the Protestant clergy as infiltrated with Communists. Eisenhower wrote a letter to a group of Catholic, Protestant and Jewish leaders denouncing that kind of attack on whole groups, and again everybody knew whom he was talking about.

He made a speech in late September of 1954 up in Boston that was a ringing endorsement of certain principles such as the fact that a country that is strong and free and confident of itself does not need people going around censoring what it can read or attempting to control its thoughts. If you read the speech, you know perfectly well he's talking about Joe McCarthy.

In November of 1953 Eisenhower gets an award from B'nai B'rith. He goes on nationwide television. He talks about the processes that you have to follow in fairness to assure the rights of citizens—a code that he remembers from his boyhood days in Abeliene. Again, an extemporaneous kind of off-the-cuff reminiscence. He kept asserting his ideas. He made very clear the types of conduct he did not like, the types of principles to which he adhered, the types of procedures which he thought the American people ought to follow.

Next, and this goes to the consensus question, Eisenhower was determined to keep his promise when he came into office: his administration would go into the government, take a look, and set up a security program. Whenever, after deliberation and adjudication, they found people who were security risks, they would eliminate them from the government. They did that. They did it conscientiously, and they did it quite vigorously.

Eisenhower was asked in November of 1953 whether he thought Communists-in-government would be an issue in the Con gressional election in November of 1954, and he said, "No." He said, "We have set up this program. We are trying to pursue it in a fair and decent manner. And I think that by November of 1954 we will have done that so thoroughly and so satisfactorily that that old issue of Communists in government is going to be a dead letter." At that moment McCarthy hit the ceiling. And in doing so he showed that Eisenhower had hit a nerve. You take that issue away from McCarthy, you take his consensus away from him, and he is dead, dead, dead.

QUESTION: I've read your book with considerable admiration, and I learned from it. I think that on the question of consensus maybe you are being too gentle with Eisenhower. He made a speech that you quote in which he says that the rights of all loyal Americans will be protected. The word loyal there troubles me because I think the rights of all Americans ought to be protected. Also, I think that Eisenhower had a chance to attack McCarthy's behavior without, in his words, getting down into the gutter with him. There were other ways for a leader with his popularity to act, and he wouldn't have had to deny that there had been Communists in the government. He wouldn't have had to argue that Hiss was not guilty.

MR. EWALD: Let me say that the sentence you read is the kind of sentence that should not have appeared in his speech. Because you are right: there is a flaw in it. There is no way you can protect only the rights of the loyal. You are trying, of course, to separate the loyal from the subversive. And beyond that, you are trying to eliminate security risks—people whose presence in the government threatens the national security of the United States. In doing so, Eisenhower and Brownell wanted to protect the rights of the accused. But they also made clear that if there were a doubt, it would be resolved in favor of the government. That is, the government has a right to protect itself. The problem had become so acute, they believed, that people were questioning the integrity of government itself. The administration had to lean over backwards to restore citizen confidence.

  Now, in the other part of your question, you said there were other things that Eisenhower could have done. I've always wondered what those other things were.

QUESTION: He had the opportunity to have made powerful statements in principle on this issue that I think the people were capable of understanding—that there was a difference between getting rid of real loyalty risks in important places and approving of McCarthy.

MR. EWALD: But he did that in the campaign in Wisconsin, with McCarthy personally present. At the first whistlestop on the morning after he skinned McCarthy alive, he said, "We know we've got a problem, we want to restore confidence in the integrity of the government, but I disagree with McCarthy on methods, and I've told him so." And McCarthy was shaking his head; he didn't like what he had heard.

Sure, Ike could have made more speeches in 1952. He could have added to what he had said about General Marshall in his press conference in August of 1952. But I would maintain that his view of McCarthy's methods and his agreement with the citizenry on the existence of a genuine problem which had to be corrected were both understood and consistent. So I fail to see what was radically wrong.

QUESTION: To continue on this point about communism, I wonder if from the advantage of hindsight we could say unintentionally both Truman and Eisenhower contributed at least to moral McCarthyism if not the brutal clumsy kind that the senator used.

If you read Harry Truman's inaugural you will find a most violent attack on some abstraction known as communism. It's not even clear what this is. You find this abstraction also in Eisenhower's inaugural. There was just never any pause to analyze what this thing meant. I don't blame them for not digging out from under that, and in fact we were all part of it, were we not? It never occurred to me to question it.

MR. EWALD: Well, I think what you are saying is, again, that you had a widespread agreement of that sort. Harry Truman started it. He certainly enunciated it. Eisenhower in some respects repeated that kind of enunciation.

I will mention, though, that a few weeks after Eisenhower's inaugural address they were trying to figure out what he ought to say to the American Society of Newspaper Editors in April just after the death of Stalin. The State Department wanted a tough speech about the evils of communism. And Emmet Hughes was in working with him, and Ike said, "Look, if I want to go to war with Russia I know where to get advice on going to war, and it is not in the State Department." He said, "I am sick and tired of the arms race, and I think it is time to try to get some kind of modus vivendi, some kind of understanding with the Soviet leaders, as bad as they are and as much as we dislike them, that will enable us somehow to turn this whole thing around." Now that is a theme Eisenhower enunciated from a standing start in the middle of this period of very, very violent hostility.

So when you are looking for a leader to break out of a pattern that's formed in the public mind, I would say Ike did it on April 16, 1953, and he continued with it. He wanted to put atomic energy in the hands of an international agency and turn atomic energy to peaceful purposes. And some people in the Pentagon said this is the equivalent of Chamberlain with his umbrella.

QUESTION: I just don't agree. His second inaugural was even worse on the Manichean contrast between our forces and communism.

QUESTION: Do you think Eisenhower recognized that with his policies a lot of people were going to get hurt? I wonder how thoughtful he was about supporting this kind of policy. Did he really think these people in government were really dangers to it? Or, like the Italian General, was he willing to lose a few people— right or wrong—in order to hold a position?

MR. EWALD: I don't think he was throwing them to the wolves. I think he really believed in the security program. They didn't see it as a loyalty program. In the first year, they had seven thousand dismissed. Of those, something like seventeen hundred and forty-three were dismissed with some kind of subversive association. And they didn't say these people were actually disloyal. They made it quite clear that these were not all Communists. They didn't identify anybody as a Communist. I believe Eisenhower believed that the program was necessary and that it was being carried forward in a reasonable and fair manner. Sure, you can find violations of fairness. Some of those hearings were incredible. Some people went to court and got reinstated. On the other hand, I think he believed in the program as a whole, believed that it did eliminate security risks and that it did in the end restore citizens' trust. And I don't think he felt that he was throwing out a few innocents along with the guilty.

In fact, after McCarthy went after the Department of the
Army, some thirty-five Army people were suspended. They went
through the Army's regular security process, and I recall that
twenty-seven or twenty-eight of them were put back on their jobs.
There was a difference between the process in the Executive
Branch and the McCarthy process of naming names.

QUESTION: I'm focusing now on Eisenhower's strategy. He
hated McCarthy. Fine. So what is he going to do about it? His
predecessor had attacked McCarthy by name and said all of
those dumb things about red herrings, and in addition Truman
was the inheritor of FDR, who, many thought, took the country
down the road to socialism and thought we could get along with
Uncle Joe Stalin after the war. FDR took Alger Hiss to Yalta, and
Truman inherited all that.

Furthermore, Truman was a failed haberdasher. He was no
hero in any sense. He lost China. He appointed a secretary of
state who wouldn't turn his back on Alger Hiss. He got us in this
no-win war in Korea. He fired Douglas MacArthur. He sur-
rounded himself with corrupt cronies and had the lowest
approval rating of any American President.

Now this man obviously was in no rhetorical position to
attack McCarthy and get away with it. He didn't have the image.
He didn't have the prestige. He didn't have the authority. In
contrast, Ike was a national hero in everybody's book. Nor was he
perceived as soft on Communists. No connection with Yalta or
appeasement. Not responsible for the fall of China. The stature
of the man was totally different from the stature of Truman.
Consequently the argument which he used against his brother
Milton—an argument which I think you accept—that he could
not frontally attack McCarthy and succeed—that argument is
totally false. I think he could have. But it need not have been a
frontal attack.

He could have done all kinds of things, such as getting Nixon
to come out front against McCarthy.

Nixon could not be outflanked on the right. We saw that later
when he went to China; no Democrat could have done that.
Eisenhower could have used Nixon in an attack on McCarthy.
He could have used General Ridgway, a national hero who hated
McCarthy's guts worse than Eisenhower did. He could even

probably have persuaded J. Edgar Hoover to attack McCarthy because we know now from the FBI files that Hoover did not like McCarthy, and Hoover was constantly fighting to keep FBI documents out of McCarthy's hands. There are a number of people in Congress Ike could have worked through: Margaret Chase Smith and others who opposed McCarthy. He did not have to expose himself by getting down in the gutter.

Now what would have happened? Even if he had not persuaded all the people out in the boondocks for whom this anti-Communist consensus was so strong, he clearly could have carried the press, and Ike himself acknowledged that it was the press that made McCarthy. Now if the press had been neutralized, if it had been clear that Eisenhower was behind the contention that McCarthy was a liar and a cheat, that would have killed him a year or a year and a half earlier than he did. Now I would like to hear your response to that.

MR. EWALD: That's a long question. Let's do the press first. I frankly find it hard to believe that any working journalist who could read did not know what Ike thought about McCarthy. I'm certain that Bill Lawrence of the *New York Times* knew; I think Bob Donovan of the *Herald Tribune* knew. They could read the speeches, and they had access to top people behind the scenes. So the argument that they didn't know, should have been informed, and would have turned one hundred and eighty degrees, I do not believe.

QUESTION: It wasn't a question of informing. It was a question of setting the pace, of making public, perhaps by surrogates, the challenge to the guy's legitimacy so that all these people who knew McCarthy was lying would have had a reason to disregard him, to cut him off as they did after the Army/McCarthy hearings.

MR. EWALD: Maybe he could have timed it differently. What Eisenhower did, however, is largely what you have suggested he should have done. He did work through surrogates, people of unexceptionable anti-Communist standing, to inform the American people of the difference between his side and the McCarthy side.

Start with the summer of 1953, the letter to the three clergymen denouncing McCarthy's staff director, J.B. Mathews, for accusing the Protestant clergy of communism. That was engineered in the White House by Emmet Hughes and on the Hill by Richard Nixon and Bill Rogers.

Later that year Attorney General Brownell made his speech saying Harry Dexter White was a Communist spy when he was appointed by Harry Truman to a big job in the International Monetary Fund. Brownell laid that out, and for a moment McCarthy lost the anti-Communist headlines.

And in the spring of 1954 three things happened. As the animosity between McCarthy and the administration intensified, Eisenhower personally designates Nixon to go on nationwide television as the administration's spokesman.

A few weeks later Brownell, with his Harry Dexter White speech in the background, goes on television to talk about the security program and the elimination of security risks from the government.

Finally, in the Army/McCarthy hearings themselves there comes a moment when J. Edgar Hoover had to stand up in public and be counted either for McCarthy or for Eisenhower. McCarthy had introduced a document written, he says, by Hoover. The committee wants to know: did he write it or didn't he? They send an emissary to ask the director. He reports what the director says: the document is a phony.

So by the end of the hearings, two of the three men you've mentioned Eisenhower did use. This deployment at the end forces the American people to decide—to answer the question: which anti-Communist side are you on? Do you side with Eisenhower, Nixon, Rogers, Brownell and Hoover? Or do you side with McCarthy? You can't waffle. You can't be on both sides.

That forcing of a choice happened on the security risk issue. It also happened on the issue of executive privilege. In the middle of the hearings Eisenhower slammed down the portcullis and shut off an endless excursion into White House documents, into Pentagon documents, and Pentagon witnesses outside the Army. We are not going to have the attorney general up there testifying, he said. We are not going to have Sherman Adams testifying. And we are not going to drag these hearings on for month after month. They are going to end right here. When Ike got to that point, people again had to stand up and be counted. And do you know whom Eisenhower was really affronting in that assertion of executive privilege? It was not in the first instance Joe McCarthy. It was John McClellan, Stuart Symington, and Scoop Jackson—three committee Democrats who would just have loved to have got into those White House files—plus the Republican members of the committee who wanted to go along.

When you reached that moment of decision, all these smart people—McClellan, Jackson, and Symington—backed off. The Republicans backed off. Right-winger Majority Leader Bill Knowland backed off from a Constitutional confrontation with Ike. The only one who continued to fight was McCarthy, all by himself, calling for people in the government to bring him any evidence they had of subversion in the executive branch. Again you had a line drawn, and people had to make a choice. And they did.

QUESTION: I follow your reasoning and I must say that I'm inclined to agree with much of it. I have two reservations.

You imply through the book and I think here today that Eisenhower had a grand strategy to overcome this problem. I have to raise my question in two parts. One, how much of this demise of McCarthyism under Eisenhower was attributable not to a grand design but to the fact that McCarthy attacked the United States Army? Suppose it had been the Internal Revenue Service or whatever. Would Eisenhower have responded with the same intensity?

Second, when the Senate challenged the Executive Branch, wasn't Eisenhower simply forced to draw the line? I mean he had no alternative.

MR. EWALD: That's a good question. I'm glad you asked it because now we can turn the page. The answer is there was no grand design. There was no masterminding. There was a lot of sheer dumb luck. Lots of accidents. Lots of stupidity. Lots of mistakes and lots of plain cussedness of human nature that entered into the whole story. I'm glad you brought that out because I think this is a mistake that people have made with this event—the opposite of the mistake of saying Ike didn't do anything, just kept himself clean. He didn't mastermind every single episode. I specifically disclaim that in the book.

Let me answer your question about the Army. I think the ball just happened to land there. If it had hit some other agency of government, I think history would have come out the same. On the executive privilege question I believe Eisenhower waited until he saw a clear-cut issue. This question of what the President can withhold and the Congress can demand is a contentious question, and if the President draws the line at the wrong place he can get himself into trouble. So he had to draw a line where he would have overwhelming public and congressional support.

But believe me, the story includes a lot of accidents along the way. Take, for example, this sequence of events in the compiling of a list of charges against McCarthy by the Army. Was this an example of Eisenhower's master strategy? Just look at the record:

Army counselor John Adams has a problem. His boss Army Secretary Bob Stevens has gone to the Far East. John Adams is faced with having to respond to McCarthy very quickly and produce witnesses. He is all alone there by himself at the Pentagon, and he is overworked and overburdened, and he yells for help from across the river at the Justice Department. He goes over and sees the Deputy Attorney General, Bill Rogers. Adams mentions all McCarthy's efforts to get special favors for Schine, and Rogers says, "Why don't you make a list of those?" Later they go into a meeting with Attorney General Brownell in Brownell's office. Sherman Adams is there, Cabot Lodge is there, Jerry Morgan is there. And during that meeting Sherman Adams also says: put together a list.

So John Adams goes back and starts to put together his chronology. He dictates recollections. He throws in memos. He produces a jumble. Anyway, he sends a copy over to Rogers and then eventually to Sherman Adams, but meanwhile he is sitting there feeling just awful, and his friends from the press come in and he leaks the whole story to them.

Meanwhile, nothing is happening at the White House. Eisenhower didn't instigate that chronology. And don't let anybody tell you he set up that meeting and masterminded the compilation of the list of events; he didn't. But then McCarthy tees off on General Zwicker. Bob Stevens tells the McCarthy committee he's not going to send any more people up there to testify. The drama is coming to a screaming climax. Stevens goes to the fried chicken lunch with McCarthy and appears to knuckle under to McCarthy's demands. Now the White House people realize: we've got this John Adams document. Let's do something with it. Lots of people already know about it. Cabot Lodge knows about it. Lucius Clay up in New York knows about it. Some reporters know about it. And by the time the people in the Pentagon, Struve Hensel and Fred Seaton, start working on John Adams' document to put it into bulletproof shape, Hensel is thinking he has to run as fast as he can before the story breaks. So his effort becomes almost defensive.

They lucked out. They did get the chronology revised before it became public knowledge. None of this sounds to me like any Eisenhower master strategy.

QUESTION: Am I correct then in inferring that your ultimate conclusion is that it was Eisenhower's known dislike or loathing of McCarthy and McCarthyism that allowed these subordinate people within the administration to play this game as they played it?

MR. EWALD: Absolutely. Sherman Adams told me in so many words: "Eisenhower never called us in and said look, here is what I want you fellows to do, I want you to go out and get McCarthy, and I want you to do it in X,Y,Z ways." But they knew what he thought about McCarthy. They knew the actions they were taking day-by-day squared with his view of McCarthy, and they knew if they misstepped he would blow the whistle on them.

Those four men—Adams, Hagerty, Seaton, Hensel—were absolutely in step. What they did, they did in Eisenhower's name.

QUESTION: With the end of World War II, with the beginning of the imperial American action with the Truman Doctrine when we took charge of the world because God had given us the atomic bomb, we had to have an ideology and identify an enemy, communism. So the whole ideology fell into place, and not just the government but every single institution in the society came into question.

So when you criticize Eisenhower for not heading directly into what had now become a hurricane, it really puts the responsibility on Eisenhower to turn around the entire cultural perception of who the enemy was. In that sense the efforts that he and various Republican people like Margaret Chase Smith made, seemed to me to be very helpful, very significant.

I remember a story I heard in confidence in Washington—I don't know whether it is true or not—about Lester Hunt, the senator from Wyoming whose son had been caught in a homosexual act. Senator Herman Welker went to him and said, "From here you are voting with McCarthy, our group," and Hunt shot himself and left a letter on his desk saying that he had spent his entire life hoping to become a senator and to serve with honesty and integrity only to get there and find that a central corruption existed in the Senate itself. That letter I was told was carried immediately to the leaders of the Democratic and Republican parties, and only then did the leadership in the Senate finally resolve that they would have to censure Mc-Carthy.

MR. EWALD: It is interesting. There is a very touching phone conversation that Lester Hunt had with Bob Stevens at the height of all this fracas. Hunt was a Democrat, and Stevens was very much moved by Hunt's solicitude. Stevens got a lot of calls from Democratic senators and congressmen and Republicans, too. Jerry Ford called him up and said, "Stay in there and fight, Bob," as he was getting slaughtered.

QUESTION: After the end of the hearings, McCarthy announced that a member of the Senate was a security risk. He was going to state who it was. Hunt went into the office and killed himself. Senator Karl Mundt came to the floor of the Senate and said, "I want to assure you that Senator Hunt is not the senator to whom McCarthy was referring." McCarthy would not say that himself.

QUESTION: Did not Eisenhower in his second term really begin the détente negotiation process?

MR. EWALD: I think that most of the people I talk to who are interested in arms control credit Eisenhower with really being a

father of SALT I and date his initiation of détente not in 1956 but
on April 16, 1953 when he addressed the American Society of
Newspaper Editors. The arms control idea came out absolutely
cold, out of the blue, and he followed it over and over again. I
don't know whether you've seen the letter that he wrote in the
spring of 1956 to the head of Simon and Schuster. Tony Lewis
has quoted it, and David Broder and a lot of other people. It is a
wonderful letter on the fact that we have got to the point where
war makes absolutely no sense and we are either going to have
the sanity to sit down and get rid of these arms and make peace
or we are going to blow ourselves up. It is a compelling letter, and
he believed this from the start. He followed this through his
administration as well as he could.

QUESTION: But he failed.

MR. EWALD: We've all failed. Haven't got there yet. Sure, I
agree.

QUESTION: I don't want to be too much like Jim Smiley's dog
here, getting hold of the hind leg and hanging on until the other
dog quits, but I do think there is a question about the consensus
here that we still haven't talked enough about. Maybe we disagree
about what the consensus was.

Truman had his own loyalty program before 1952. Also, it was
his Justice Department, however reluctantly or however much
goaded by Nixon, that prosecuted Alger Hiss. So there was some
basis for not making this the completely partisan issue that it
became by the 1952 campaign. And the very choice of Richard
Nixon as the vice-presidential nominee indicated that Eisenhower and his team were wiling to use this supposed consensus,
to heighten it by making this a major issue in the campaign.

The real question, I think, between those of us who disagree
and you, Mr. Ewald, is what Eisenhower might have done earlier
to shape this consensus or to stop it from getting worse. It didn't
just begin with McCarthy in 1950. It had been going on for two or
three years at least and very intensely before the conviction of
Hiss.

You mentioned in your book a speech—you call it a brilliant
speech—that Nixon gave. I was a partisan. I am a partisan. I
remember hearing Nixon give that speech. I remember the part

that you quote that a Communist traitor is like a rat and you shoot him. Then he did go on to attack McCarthy but he was not resisting the notion that these are rats out there and we've got to do something dreadful about them. So it isn't simply a speech that is in favor of civil liberties.

But the larger issue of the consensus still remains. I think it was more up for influence by a leader in 1952 and 1953.

MR. EWALD: I guess what I would say is that I think the Eisenhower people did see the possibility of subversion as a major issue. I think they saw it as an issue that had to be dealt with, and the only way you could really deal with it was to bring new management into the government, institute some kind of scrutiny of the government which people would respect and believe was genuine—not a stonewalling or whitewashing—and solve the real problem. It couldn't be done by making speeches.

QUESTION: Yes, but I thought we agreed that the Truman administration had a loyalty program. You say that in the book.

MR. EWALD: They did. And they kicked people out. In fact, they kicked out many of the old China hands. But the point is that they undermined their credibility by their defensiveness—by talking about red herrings and refusing to turn away from Hiss.

QUESTION: Suppose Eisenhower had chosen someone from the Taft wing who was not the most prominent figure in the anti-Communist or witch hunting movement. Suppose he had chosen somebody respectable, clearly anti-Communist but not the best noted person on the Un-American Activities Committee. Could he not have accomplished the same thing? The question is whether this consensus forced him to do that or whether he contributed to the consensus by the choices that he made in 1952. And I think the latter, obviously.

MR. EWALD: I think it is possible, although I think Nixon was clearly distinguished in the minds of most people from

McCarthy. And he was chosen not only because of his record in the House Committee but also because of geography, youth and his acceptability to the Taft wing. Whom were you going to put in there from the Taft wing? The great problem with setting up that ticket was to keep the Taft people from walking out.

QUESTION: He could have taken Bob Taft himself.

MR. EWALD: He wouldn't have taken Bob Taft, he couldn't have, no one would have accepted him, and there were a bunch of other Taftites who were absolutely anathema to the Eisenhower people. But Nixon was acceptable. He was acceptable to the Taft people; he was acceptable to the Eisenhower people; he was sufficiently distanced from McCarthy. And you may be right, that that choice tilted the Republican direction a bit. I wouldn't deny that.

QUESTION: You talked, as so many new writers on Eisenhower have, about the fact that he was trying to lead the country off in a new direction, and you referred several times to the April 1953 speech before the American Society of Newspaper Editors, which was a magnificent speech. But you have not talked about the speech that Dulles made to that same group on that same day, which was an entirely different speech moving in an entirely different direction.

Now I wonder if you read the *State Department Bulletin*.

MR. EWALD: I wouldn't say that I've read every page. I've read a lot of pages in the *State Department Bulletin.*

QUESTION: I thought if you had read it you would know exactly what I'm going to say. Now the *State Department Bulletin* is the crucial statement of the State Department on national policy, and it reflects public statements made by high Executive Branch officials across the country, and those speeches appeared in the press and created far more comment than anything Eisenhower ever said.

Now when you read the *State Department Bulletin*, let's take the subject of liberation. Liberation never ceased. In fact we end up with talk about "captive nations" late in 1959,

which indicates we are building up, not going down, on
liberation.

On China we were also going up, not down. The attacks on
China never died down, and finally by 1959 Assistant Secretary
of State for Far Eastern Affairs Walter Robertson in a speech in
Canada said that Mao is no more important to China than
William Z. Foster is to the United States. Now you can't get any
farther than that.

And then let's get on to Indochina and all the commitments to
Indochina all through the fifties, making in my estimation the
war in Vietnam quite impossible to avoid.

MR. EWALD: What commitments? Made when?

QUESTION: In speech after speech. Just read the *State Department Bulletin*, just one after another.

MR. EWALD: You mean a binding commitment?

QUESTION: Well, as much as words can do it.

MR. EWALD: Well, there is a difference.

QUESTION: That is the point I want to make. Those words are
what I read. Those words are what the world reads, and I think
that gets down to my final question about Eisenhower, the
moderate, sensible man, the man whose personal letters are
simply brilliant and wonderful. I've read them in the Eisenhower
Library. They show so much sensibility. But how does one as an
historian deal with that and deal with all those public statements
I've mentioned in which the commitments and the words are
getting more and more extreme as the administration goes on?
Now that's the question. I'm delighted I posed that question
because I don't meet many people like you.

MR. EWALD: Let's take the question on Vietnam because that
has become obviously a bone of contention. I remember in the
late summer of 1965 I got a phone call up in Connecticut. It was a
warm Saturday afternoon. The caller said, "I'm down here at the
White House, and I work for Bill Bundy and I understand you've

been reading these papers, these documents in Eisenhower's office in Gettysburg." He said, "I'd just like to ask a simple question: Why are we in Vietnam?" Now when that phone call came in, we were very close to having four or five hundred thousand troops in there. So I thought, with half a million people, you ought to know why you are there. And I said, "Why are you asking me?" He said, "I want to know whether there was a secret commitment made by Eisenhower to Diem during the fifties that would really bind the United States." I said, "Look, you know as much as I do. I've looked all through those papers. I've never seen a secret letter or a secret commitment."

Now by this time this issue had become public. Lyndon Johnson had got up and said that what we were doing in Vietnam wasn't something new, it went back several administrations, Republican and Democratic, and it went back to Eisenhower. He was really trying to name Dwight Eisenhower as the originator through some kind of binding commitment. And Eisenhower denied having made any kind of commitment that would tie the hands of either his administration or of future administrations in Southeast Asia. So that is why I bridled a bit at the word commitment. I will not deny that we helped Diem. We gave him economic aid. We had military advisors in there. We sent them money and we did all kinds of things and tried to make him promise to clean up the government. They instituted land reform, for example.

But something that really locked us into a policy—to my knowledge, it never did exist.

QUESTION: Well, it never existed later either. There never was a document—there never was. We fought the war without it.

MR. EWALD: Of course. That's the whole ludicrous point. The guy hung up the phone, and he had to go back and report we've got no commitment. They didn't have one, and they were looking for us to provide one for them.

Your other question is interesting about the words and the conflict. I think when you look at Eisenhower, it is very easy to lean in one direction or another. Eisenhower is not a pacifist, not a hundred percent disarmer. Eisenhower is a centrist. He goes down the center. He's got advisers on one side. He's got advisers

on the other. He calls them in. They disagree. He'll follow this
one, he'll follow that one, and he improvises. And so I would
have no doubt that Walter Robertson was continuing to be just as
bellicose over there in the State Department as he was, and
Foster Dulles also tended to lean toward bellicosity at times.
Mention has been made of the 1957 inaugural address, which in
a way was a very generous address. It talked a lot about the Third
World and the winds of change and so on. But there was also, I'm
sure, quite a hardline anti-communism running through it. So I
won't say that you won't find evidence on both sides of that line.
As you say, the State Department speechwriters get started with a
theme, and they will just continue to hit that theme and hit it and
hit it and hit it. But you will find that the policy is not
unrelievedly of that sort; that you have on the other side
initiatives that Eisenhower made or tried to make that he did
believe in that were conciliatory.

During the 1956 campaign, for example, he had a long
correspondence with Chester Bowles about the issues in the
campaign. They agreed on a lot of things, and he wrote back to
Bowles and said, "I have no hesitation in saying that I agree with
you about a lot of things but just don't you go out and try to use
this politically against me in the forthcoming election."

He enunciated a desire to begin the process of détente, and
he would talk about it to generals and military officers in
conference when he was really trying to get them to see that the
big problem was not how to fight the next war but how to avoid
war. He really believed that. And on the other hand if you look at
his administration and the technology of defense you see an
enormous cornucopia of one thing after the other—of nuclear
weapons and missiles and satellites and U2s and the follow-on to
the U2.

So I would say that he was going down the center line. Some
of the things that I've mentioned fall on one side and the things
you mentioned fall on the other, and Eisenhower was somewhere
in the middle. He was very tough on communism, and at the
same time he was a man with great common sense, and blatant
military jingoism he had no use for. I think that is really where
you have to come out. Does that make sense?

QUESTION: Well, yes it does and I appreciate your answer. The
rhetoric around the administration was very extremist. I know

that it was not Eisenhower's. But why did he permit all this extremist language—this cold war, anti-Soviet, anti-Chinese rhetoric? What's the importance of the rhetoric? Well, the rhetoric does a lot. Take Vietnam for example. What got us involved there? It wasn't a commitment, it was a rhetoric.

If you talk often enough about falling dominos, ultimately in a crunch you can't escape the concept of falling dominos, and I don't see how Eisenhower could have escaped it if he had remained President. He had mentioned falling dominos so many times. Like that speech at Gettysburg in 1959. It was a beautiful statement of falling dominos. But you know when you had said that over and over again, and the chips were down and things began to fall in 1961, Kennedy was trapped. But I don't know just how anybody would have escaped, really.

MR. EWALD: My favorite expression of falling dominoes in early 1954 is not Eisenhower's but Hubert Humphrey's and Paul Douglas'. They said the dominoes would fall all the way from Southeast Asia to Ireland in one direction and all the way to the Philippines in the other. People really did believe in the domino theory, and I think they believed it because of Munich. You try to find somebody who said Chamberlain was right at Munich. They would have ridden him out of town.

QUESTION: The question is did Ike know all this stuff was coming out of the State Department?

MR. EWALD: Sure. Of course. Remember the Quemoy-Matsu issue in both 1954 and 1958. Eisenhower kind of waffled between two extremes—intervention and retreat—and didn't get to the place Nixon got to in the 1960 debates with Kennedy: draw the line and don't yield one square inch of free territory. Eisenhower was smart enough never to do that.

QUESTION: In a speech at the time of Dienbienphu, Nixon was saying we had to stop the fall there, and Eisenhower did nothing about it.

MR. EWALD: Read the book. Nixon got off the reservation. The administration repudiated the statement the next day. It is very easy to look back on Eisenhower and say he kept us out of Vietnam. I'm very happy that people like that interpretation, but you have to qualify it. Eisenhower in fact wanted us to go into Vietnam in 1954. But he wanted us to go in under certain conditions: with a big international alliance; with native troops fighting on the ground, not Americans down there in the jungle; with an announcement by the French that they would get out of there and let the country become independent. All those conditions that Ike wanted, he could never put together. So he said, "Forget it. I'm not going in." And he worried. He worried about what was happening over there. But he had the courage to turn his back on an unacceptable set of circumstances.

Another example. You could say Dulles was tough. Well, Dulles was pretty tough, but Dulles and Eisenhower together went over every foreign policy speech either one of them gave. Eisenhower operated that way in many areas of the government. Take, for instance, a little-known speech made by Air Force Secretary Donald Quarles in early 1956 called, "How Much Is Enough?" That speech argued for nuclear sufficiency—not superiority, not getting way ahead of the Russians in the arms race, but having enough for an assured second strike. And you know that policy was the Eisenhower policy. You get into the 1960 election and what happens to that policy? It becomes portrayed as the policy of a tired old man who doesn't really want to be first anymore in the world, who wants just to save money, to keep the defense budget from getting too high. Forget that! his critics say. We are going to be first. We are going to spend what we have to spend.

Basically that kind of restraint damaged Eisenhower's reputation for a long time. And so there were conciliatory speeches coming out of the Pentagon as well as some bellicose ones coming out of the State Department.

QUESTION: On the military policy you are right. There is an enormous amount of restraint that makes Eisenhower look very good.

MR. EWALD: On the subject of arms control, certainly you got to a crunch in the summer of 1957 where Harold Stassen was over in London negotiating. People who were with him then and who believe in what he was doing thought he really had made some movements of progress. Then all of a sudden he made a mistake: he went directly to the Russians with a proposal without adequately notifying the British and blew the whole thing out of the water. Well, that was too bad. And maybe things would have been different if that negotiation had not failed.

QUESTION: I regret dropping this to the lower level of security and loyalty risks. I believe you said the administration, when it made announcements, made very clear the difference between security risks and loyalty risks.

Now, that was forced by actions in the Congress. I was a clerk then to a senior member of the House Appropriations Committee. When an appropriations bill came up, the general counsel of the Treasury announced that they had fired one hundred and six people as security risks. He attempted to explain that you could be a security risk without being disloyal. For example, he said, you could be an alcoholic or have a relative behind the Iron Curtain. One congressman who had a relative in Poland said, "You are not going to get out of this room alive. Call the cops. No one is going to call me a security risk and get out of this room alive."

As a result of that particular hearing they had to come up with a breakdown. And they came back and said that of the one hundred and six people that we discharged as security risks, three had loyalty problems. As a result the administration, which had been gloriously going on saying we found all these thousands of security risks, had to make the separation.

QUESTION: Let me turn to the leadership question again.

I appreciated the earlier observation that rhetoric does a lot; perhaps the perceived absence of rhetoric can do a lot too. What I really like about your book was that it does focus the judgment of Ike's leadership on his standard of prudence. You do portray him as someone who did not wander too far from the center. A President has lots of issues, he has finite moral capital to spend on them, and it may have been prudent of Ike to reserve some of his moral capital for something other than McCarthy. Maybe we can accuse him of saving it up too much. I would just like to know whether you think his judgment on that was a balanced one.

MR. EWALD: I think he used his personal assets, whatever they were, where he thought they would do some good. He made speeches about principles and right conduct. But he thought to stand up and make a speech doing the one thing that he didn't do—inserting in the blank the name of Senator Joseph R. McCarthy of Wisconsin—that I think he felt would have been counterproductive, bad strategy even for him. As a friend of mine said, he didn't hit people, because when you hit people the sympathy of the public goes to the hittee, and McCarthy would have been the hittee. Eisenhower made very clear what he thought about McCarthy, but a personal confrontation he really felt would not work. I don't think he was saying I've got only so many nickels here that I can use. I think he really believed in his strategy.

QUESTION: Was he wrong?

MR. EWALD: I don't think so. He exercised the options that came open to him at particular moments, let events proceed, and at the climactic moment of the hearings, asserted his executive privilege. This was a very damaging blow to McCarthy. It isolated him. You had nearly everybody in the United States on one side of the line with the President, including all the committee Democrats and the committee Republicans, and Joe all by himself on the other.

QUESTION: But I gather that these other gentlemen disagree with you. They think Ike could have done it earlier and got away with it.

MR. EWALD: People have said this time and again. They said Eisenhower should have made a speech saying: "Look, McCarthy is a liar, there are no Communists in government, it's all a witchhunt, it's nonsense, let's forget it and get rid of this crazy actor from Wisconsin." And they argue that in five minutes McCarthy would have been a dead duck. I don't believe that.

QUESTION: I recently read a new biography of Herbert Hoover, and it concentrates on his last post-presidential years. To my astonishment I found that when the subversion issue first developed, President Truman wrote to his new friend, Mr. Hoover, and requested Hoover to head up a bipartisan commission. Hoover wrote back—and I think this puts this matter of consensus in a somewhat more complicated manner—that the issue was not the few Communists that may be in the government. The real issue was: who in the government had attempted to force our policy toward the Russian side? And that if he headed the commission it would have to make a broad investigation into that question. Of course that ended it.

Now my question. How, in your view, are we now to interpret the military-industrial complex speech? Are we to interpret it as a warning against a complex which threatens our control of foreign policy—a rational foreign policy in the future? Or are we to interpret it as meaning simply that the power of procurement by the military had created an alliance with the industrial element of the society which was going to make it impossible for us to have a rational budget in the future?

Which do you think he meant?

MR. EWALD: I think probably a little bit of both, to tell you the truth. I don't think his concern was just confined to the federal budget. If you go back to May of 1953, he made a talk about national security and its costs. Basically he said that we disarmed after World War II, then armed to our teeth during Korea, with spending way up. Now it's coming down after Korea. And what we have to do is to keep it on a level steadily, and he did, at about forty billion dollars, without vast increases and with great effectiveness, especially technological effectiveness. That was the budgetary side. In addition, he always said there was only one way to have total security and that was to go to a garrison state, and if you go to a garrison state—and he used these words early in his administration, 1953—if you go to a garrison state, forget about civil liberties and forget about your rights, forget about a peacetime economy, and go armed to the teeth in readiness to fight a war. He said, "We don't want to do that." And I'm sure in the 1961 farewell address, he was thinking the same kind of thing, about our ability to function as a society—not just have a good foreign policy, but to conduct the kind of society that we really hope to have. So he believed you have to keep this possible threat under very tight scrutiny and control.

Now there were certain things he always feared might swell this defense component in the society, and one of them was presidential ignorance of the process. He told his military assistants, "Someday there is going to be sitting in this office a man who doesn't understand—when somebody from the Pentagon comes in and says we need this weapons system—whether they need it or not, whether it's good, bad, or indifferent." He will be incapable, Eisenhower believed, of judging among the contending demands of this military and industrial crowd. Ike was afraid of that, and he spent most of his time on national security.

Let me point out the other thing that he mentioned in that same farewell speech: that he did not want the country to come under the control of a scientific and technological elite either. He was thinking of weapons technology, of a small group of wizards who would come in and be running the country.

QUESTION: Can you comment a bit on the documents McCarthy used in the hearings?

MR. EWALD: This is very interesting. When the Army released its charges against McCarthy, McCarthy phoned Fred Seaton in the Pentagon and said, "You really shouldn't put out those charges because we've got a lot of documents over here that refute them. My people have been instructed to keep careful records of all of their conversations with people in the Pentagon. I'll send you one of these documents just as a sample. We are searching the files for more." Well, the Army went ahead and put out its charges anyway, and very shortly thereafter McCarthy, instead of filing a set of charges, released eleven memoranda purportedly going back several months, to late 1953. Those eleven memoranda—from Frank Carr to McCarthy and Roy Cohn to McCarthy, and McCarthy to these staff men—outlined their position at the time particular events occurred and appeared to validate their claim that the Army had been holding Schine as a hostage in order to get McCarthy to call off his hearings.

So these eleven memoranda hit the press and become the

foundation for McCarthy's charges against the Army. As the Army starts to study them, slowly a light begins to go on. First John Adams and then other people look at them and say they don't sound right, and the suspicion begins to grow that they really are not genuine, that they are forgeries—that McCarthy has hinged his whole case on forged documents. When Joe Welch and Jim St. Clair came down from Boston to start work on the case, St. Clair told me, "We were convinced from the beginning that they were phonies." So they go to work trying to get solid evidence that will demonstrate the falseness. For example, one memorandum, dated at a particular time and place, was supposed to be signed by McCarthy. St. Clair was sure that McCarthy at that particular moment was not in this place, that he was on a flight out to Wisconsin. St. Clair phones the airline, and tries to get the passenger list; it had been destroyed. In short, they could never put together any kind of hard evidence that would really nail the falseness of those documents.

I'll just say in passing there was no way to authenticate them by technical tests—by analyzing the typing, for example.

So throughout the hearings Joe Welch keeps pressing the people who supposedly dictated the memoranda and the woman who typed them, Joe McCarthy's personal secretary, who incidentally is the sister of David Brinkley. I talked to her, by the way. She is living far from the public eye. So, as I was saying, Welch gets to the absolute verge of accusing the people on McCarthy's side of having forged the documents but never can really destroy them on it.

Now, a few years ago Professor Thomas Reeves wrote a biography of McCarthy saying he knew the documents were, in fact, forged. He had been told by a "McCarthy confidant" who wanted to remain anonymous. So I began to ask myself: who was this unidentified informant? Did Reeves talk to Roy Cohn? Frank Carr? He couldn't have talked to McCarthy, but did he talk to Don Surine, one of the McCarthy people? Could Surine have told him? I didn't know.

Then a year or so ago a book by Professor David Oshinsky comes out on McCarthy, and it carries this story a step further. He says he knew these documents were forged; his information came from Willard Edwards of the *Chicago Tribune*, a confidant of the McCarthy side who actually "witnessed their panicked production." In addition, Oshinsky said, he had heard from Edwards another strange thing: that not only McCarthy but also the Army forged documents; that in fact McCarthy forged some of his documents to respond to the Army forgeries. So Oshinsky prints all this and leaves the charge hanging there, a real cliffhanger.

I looked Willard Edwards up in the Washington phone book and discovered he was alive and well and living about two blocks from the Library of Congress up on Capitol Hill. And so I called him up and I said, "We met a long time ago; can I come to see you?" So I went to his home and asked him about the Reeves and Oshinsky accounts. "I am the source for both of them," he said. "Reeves respected my confidence. I told him I didn't want to be quoted, and he didn't quote me. But Oshinsky cited my name." And I said, "Well, what did you actually see?" He said, "The way I remember it is that I walked into the Congressional Hotel up there on Capitol Hill, a kind of hideaway office for McCarthy, and found a whole bunch of stenographers typing madly away, and I asked, 'What's going on?' And they said, 'We're forging documents,' or something to that effect." Edwards said he talked to Frank Carr, who was overseeing the whole process, making sure, for example, that they used paper contemporaneous with the dates they were putting on the backdated memoranda. And Willard Edwards was furious that all this had gone public with his name on it.

Oshinsky, in his book, had cited a Willard Edwards memorandum containing some of this information. This would seem to add some weight to the allegations Oshinsky reported.

And Edwards said to me, "I'll show you that document. In fact I'll give you the whole file." I carried it home with me. I opened it up, and it was nothing but a loose set of notes that Edwards had typed up toward a book he was going to write. And in one of his typed notes he recalled a conversation in Washington with a lawyer he identified as a high up Pentagon lawyer who, at a cocktail party two years after the hearings, had said, "We knew McCarthy was forging documents because they responded to documents forged by the Army." Edwards said, "I couldn't believe that this got into print; it was very irresponsible to go out with no further evidence and make this kind of accusation against the Army." Edwards said he himself had tried to validate the lawyer's allegation. He had gone back to him several days after the cocktail party and said, "You know what you told me at that party? Would you give me some more evidence? It's a very hot thing that you are saying," and the man clammed up, refused to say anything more about it. There Edwards dropped it.

So when I came to this point in the book here's where the evidence stood in the public record: McCarthy was accused of having forged documents by somebody who had witnessed the process—Willard Edwards, not anybody in the McCarthy organization itself. Second, the Army had a big forgery question mark hanging over its head.

If you had gone through the Army documents, you would know perfectly well that the Army didn't forge any documents. They never made *any* documents public before McCarthy came back with his alleged response to their alleged forgeries. Even in the hearings themselves, most of the Army's documents never saw the light of day. The Army never used them. So the conclusion that the Army forged the documents and then kept them hidden away—that conclusion to me was absolutely absurd. I tried to straighten all this out.

QUESTION: You didn't interview this former FBI agent, Mr. Carr?

MR. EWALD: He was dead.

QUESTION: So the documentary basis for this is Edwards' written recollection two years afterwards, which Edwards showed to you?

MR. EWALD: Edwards showed me what he had written down at least two years afterwards, and it was very skimpy. He then recalled for me, thirty years afterward, some more details. And who knows what the exact truth is? But at any rate he did identify Carr, and describe his own role, which was not that of a participant but that of an observer of the typing process.

Of course all this brings up the responsibility of the press. What should Willard Edwards have done, knowing what he knew? You also see other reporters in the corners of various participants. Scotty Reston offered to help Bob Stevens at least once. Certainly Arthur Hadley was a great friend of Stevens' who helped write statements for him, and was in his home working with him at the same time Hadley was the White House correspondent for *Newsweek*. Phil Potter of the *Baltimore Sun* spent a lot of time in John Adams' office listening to Adams' problems off the record and doing what he could to help. And then up on the Hill you have Willard Edwards in there with the McCarthy people.

QUESTION: And George Sokolsky and a whole bunch of others.

MR. EWALD: Sokolsky of course came in, that's right. I will say that I think Willard Edwards, when I talked with him, really wanted the correct story to come out, and I think he felt pretty bad about the way things had turned out.

QUESTION: I wonder if I could raise a general question that has come up every time we have had any group who talked about consensus. It seems to me that maybe this underlies some of the differences, maybe it doesn't, maybe it's inadequate, but if it is you may be able to point to some other things that do explain some of the differences of points of view. It's a little bit like the debate that has gone on with regard to public opinion. One school says public opinion is out there, you can identify it, measure it, test it, trace changes in it, and it is a quantity that one can study and examine.

The other view is that it's an intangible, amorphous, ever-changing factor, that leadership really determines what consensus is, and that you can't put your hand on it. You've got to change it very gradually, but you've got an imperceptible change.

The night before last people sensed that in the last few minutes of the debate Reagan tired and Mondale seemed to reach his peak. When they interviewed the people the next night in the nursing homes or old age homes, nobody said he had switched, but they expressed some doubts. They hadn't realized there was that much difference between the older man and the young man. Somebody else gives it another point. I talked to Paul Duke this morning, and he said that the thing you've got to watch so closely is what happens on Thursday and then what happens on foreign policy. And if you had a compounded series of things of this kind then you might get a fairly substantial shift, whether it changed the election results or not. But it is in flux and it is constantly subject to people writing on leadership and political science. What I wondered was, do the differences that have emerged this morning reflect two quite different views of how consensus is formed and developed, what its qualities are, and its elements, ingredients, and how it changes? Or do we all mean the same thing when we talk about consensus and its formation? I don't know.

QUESTION: I believe a leader can affect what people do. I do believe it is possible for an articulate spokesman in simple language to explain to people fairly complicated things. So really what I said about Eisenhower today comes partly from that. I think that if the people could have understood it in 1954, they could have understood it in 1952.

QUESTION: Since you looked at me as a sociologist here, I will just mention one related concept, of the moral entrepreneur. It has been applied by a sociologist to McCarthy and his type of activity: taking an issue which is somewhat dormant, getting hold of it and getting it before the public in such a way that it looks like a consensus. I don't know if you should call that leadership.

QUESTION: As I read these documents, the McCarthy people seem to have this breathless sense of discovery as if, gosh, here's this threat that no one else has ever quite seen as well as we do. As long as McCarthy was in a position to keep injecting the sense of fresh discovery I think that Ike was constrained.

QUESTION: I think also in the book you see an example of the difficulty, historically, of interpreting such things. There is a very good accounting in the book of the Edward R. Murrow broadcast. We all assume that it was the McCarthy hearings and Eisenhower's behavior and certainly Joe Welch's treatment in the hearing that did McCarthy in. We don't really know that the Murrow program didn't have more effect because you had

McCarthy there with that nervous giggle and Murrow exposing him in a vehement way. We've never measured how the people responded—how much was a response to what they saw in McCarthy, and how much was a response to the Communists' having been cleaned out.

MR. EWALD: I think that's true.

QUESTION: If I remember McCarthy, after the Senate censured McCarthy, whenever he rose on the floor of the Senate to speak, every senator left the floor. No man would stay on the floor to listen to anything he said. Moreover, when they would meet him in the tunnel from the Senate Office Building going to the Senate floor, and he would say, "Hi, Senator," they would simply walk by and not speak to him. I think, partly as a result of that, if I remember correctly, Jimmy Reston, then the head of the *New York Times* bureau in Washington, called a meeting of the chiefs of the twenty top bureaus there in which they discussed how they would report the behavior of the Senator. And from there on, in unison, they simply chopped him to ribbons.

And several people said to me: As a result of the manner in which he is being ostracized in the Senate, he is drunk all the time, every night in the week, and it is going to kill him.

QUESTION: And people began to talk about how he looked when they saw him. He looked more and more dissipated.

QUESTION: What is the timing of the censure vote, the month and the year?

MR. EWALD: It was December 2, 1954, although the hearings on the censure motion had taken place all during the fall. But the thing that impressed me as I've said, was this: I walked into the White House in July of 1954, about a month after the hearings ended, and thereafter nobody in the White House to my knowledge spent any time on McCarthy, and McCarthy's influence and popularity, his appeal around the country, didn't come up at all. And we were going through a series of congressional elections, and just a year earlier McCarthy had forecast that in those elections Communism in government would be the key issue. But it didn't arise.

I've always thought that once McCarthy lay flat on the floor, face down, the Senate could act. Even so, some voted against censure, and some didn't vote at all. One of them was Jack Kennedy, very obviously, and he later on said that he regretted his nonvote. But he still thought a vote for censure would poison him in Massachusetts. Nonetheless, McCarthy was a dead duck, I think, by the summer of 1954. And everything that happened after that was rather pathetic.

I had a nice letter from Senator Stuart Symington the other day, and he had read the book. Stuart Symington in a sense was not on the Eisenhower side. He was a Democrat on the Committee, and he stuck his neck out. But he couldn't have been more gracious about the book. And I had known that after McCarthy's censure he'd be sitting there on the floor of the Senate, and McCarthy would come over to him and put his arm around him. And Symington said, "I couldn't just turn away from him. He was a human being, after all, and I felt sorry for him."

Even John Adams was invited by McCarthy, some time after the hearings, to come over to his house and have a drink. And Adams said, "Joe you can't be serious. My wife would never set foot in your house." And McCarthy said, "These women, they take all these things so seriously." So he was a pathetic figure, I'd say, during those last years. Without question people lost interest in him. Certainly the press did. If the press had set out to lose interest in him earlier and to report both sides instead of just the McCarthy charges—say, two, three, four years earlier—they might have had an influence on the results earlier.

Eisenhower always felt that McCarthy played to the press and that the press waltzed with him because he sold newspapers and made page one headlines all the time. And Eisenhower rather resented that in the press. But you'd have to say, the press is supposed to report the news. They made a news judgment: McCarthy was big news.

QUESTION: There is a hardcore radical right—about twenty percent of the electorate, groups like the John Birch Society—which never disappears. Any time there is any trauma sufficient to activate that radical twenty percent so that they draw adherents from the center, you have got a problem. And the fact that we don't have one right now may well be due to the fact that there is that guy on horseback who is in the White House, who is standing tall in the saddle, who has made all this noise about how we have rebuilt our strength now and we can look them in the eye, and force them to back down and come to the bargaining table and sign some agreements. If we had a Democrat in there, particularly a Democrat who had been making noises about how we ought really to have détente, there would be more of a fuss, and that hard core radical right would have attracted to it a lot of people who presently are quiescent.

MR. EWALD: You know, it's interesting to think about that resurgence of suspicion. The last time this kind of problem might have arisen, I think, was during the Kennedy years. When Ronald Reagan is presiding, you certainly aren't going to have anybody screaming over an administration honeycombed with Communists. Similarly I think Jimmy Carter, given his background, probably would be spared much of that; Jerry Ford also, and Richard Nixon, and Lyndon Johnson. But in Kennedy's time, you might very well have had such a resurgence. As a matter of fact, I remember during those years some people were playing around with the idea that maybe somebody down there in State is subverting the government. This idea never got very far. But that was the period when it might have surfaced. To be sure, the Goldwater campaign of 1964 touched on it a bit. But I really don't think this mood came anywhere close to the mood of the early fifties and late forties.

QUESTION: I was interested in your statistics of only seven percent believing there were no spies in the government. I think you might get that same answer today; people have become more sophisticated about realizing there are spies. We know, for example, that they went up very high in the British intelligence.

MR. EWALD: I think that's true. Any good intelligence organization is going to try to penetrate the other side. We are probably doing that to the best of our ability.

QUESTION: Sure. Eisenhower spoke up when the U-2 was shot down. He took responsibility for it as though it were a very unusual thing, but now it is pretty well understood.

MR. EWALD: The KGB is always trying to infiltrate our government. That's their job. I don't think people worry inordinately about that. I think they worry only when they think subversion may have got out of control, or they think people in power are not paying attention or are aiding and abetting it. That became the problem in the forties and fifties.

QUESTION: For a long time China was perceived as one of the instigators of the dominoes' falling in Asia. The fact that now they are not doing that very much perhaps helps the peace.

MR. EWALD: That's interesting about China. You know, when Nehru came to the United States to visit with Eisenhower in December of 1956, they had a whole bunch of talks; they went out to the farm and walked around and conversed at great length. And they talked about China. Nehru said that it was terrible that the United States felt so anti-Chinese. Eisenhower agreed that was a bad thing but said it was a red hot, very sensitive issue particularly while the Chinese held American prisoners from Korea and were perceived as being part of the Soviet bloc. But he said if it were possible to do a few things to improve this relationship, that would be wonderful for both sides.

I don't know whether you remember that back in 1957 or 1958 for the first time the United States validated the passports of thirty American correspondents with major news organizations for travel in the People's Republic of China. As I recall, the Chinese let only one man in. He had a nice trip out of it. But they really didn't reciprocate; possibly they thought that opening the door for these journalists might put the camel inside the tent. This is a good example of how you have to work both with our public opinion and with the other side.

QUESTION: Would you say, Mr. Ewald, that Ike was actually playing a kind of double role in foreign policy? We've heard a rather repellent case against the militant rhetoric of John Foster Dulles. I have had the impression, however, that Dulles was actually more moderate, more realistic than he sounded, and that Dulles' strategy was this: He sought always to give something to the radical right within the Republican party in order to pursue the kind of semi-moderate cause, shall we say, that the administration was committed to, and that Ike apparently gave this his blessing. Is that your judgment?

MR. EWALD: Well, Eisenhower did give his blessing to what Foster Dulles did and said. They were very close. They collaborated and coordinated.

QUESTION: Yes, but there was such a difference between Dulles' rhetoric and Ike's, and we are told that Ike read everything that Dulles said and vice versa. So how do you explain this discrepancy?

MR. EWALD: I think probably that the difference lies in shadings and degree. Eisenhower could also be very tough in his rhetoric, and then he could be conciliatory. Dulles mirrored the Eisenhower foreign policy, which as I've tried to say was a mixture of things—a very tough determination not to yield to a hostile adversary; and at the same time an effort to see what you could do to make relations better, and open things up and so on. That mixture was fundamental to both of them, although certainly Dulles hit the bellicose side harder than Eisenhower did much of the time. But I think there were those two components in the policy, and so you have two men doing slightly different things but basically in consonance. I don't know whether that's a good answer, but I've never accepted the idea that Eisenhower was a man of peace going one way and Dulles was a man of war going another. I just don't think that is true.

QUESTION: Well, I don't either.

MR. EWALD: Take, for example, disarmament. Ambassador Gerard Smith is one of the gang of four urging a no-first-strike policy, the architect of Salt I and a real expert in the field. He served as Foster Dulles' assistant. He admired Eisenhower; he understood how these two men worked together. He once told me, "Dulles went along with the idea of disarmament but really felt that he was largely going through the motions, because he didn't really believe in it." But he did cooperate. Eisenhower obviously did believe in disarmament if you could do it, but past a point he would not take certain disarmament steps if they entailed a weakening of our defenses. So the two men had that kind of difference, I think, as well as an enormous difference in personality, quite obviously. But it probably made Eisenhower feel better to know that he had this no-nonsense man back at the State Department running things, and could therefore lean into the wind toward accommodation.

In 1958 Eisenhower wanted to make a speech—it would still be a good idea—offering to bring ten thousand students from the Soviet Union to United States universities, and send ten thousand Americans over there. He wanted a vast exchange of persons, a great big movement. And he said, "I get sick and tired of talking to Gromyko and all these old men set in their ways." He said, "Let's get the kids over here. Let the Americans learn something about the Soviet Union, and let the Russians come over here and learn something about this country, and we'll pay for it all." He went to J. Edgar Hoover and asked, "Is this proposal going to pose any kind of a domestic security problem?" Hoover said, "Absolutely not. It's a great idea." Then Ike went to Foster Dulles, and Dulles shot that thing down, threw cold water all over it. You can see what happened when this fresh idea went through the State Department meat grinder. And it made Ike furious, and he bridled and complained, and he ground his teeth. Milton Eisenhower powerfully favored the plan, and he and Arthur Larson helped draft the speech. Eisenhower couldn't convince Dulles. And so he said: Okay, if that's what they want, the whole thing is off. He deferred to Dulles' judgment. I think this is a rather good illustration of how they worked together. Ike wasn't going to fire his secretary of state, and override him. He respected him but disagreed with him. And a tough attitude killed off a very peaceful and imaginative initiative.

Incidentally, this happened in the spring of 1958, right after Sputnik had gone up. Everybody else was saying, "How are we going to get up there and beat the Russians in space?" And Eisenhower was wondering about the students, close to his heart.

QUESTION: I would like to ask whether Ike could have created a consensus around the proposition that while it is necessary to oppose Communism, to keep security risks out of the government, we can do so without sacrificing civil liberties? He made public statements to this effect, and so presumably he was behind this kind of anti-McCarthy consensus. The fact that he did not attempt seriously to foster such a consensus—that I hold against him.

MR. EWALD: I think that is exactly what he was trying to do.

QUESTION: How?

MR. EWALD: I think he tried to do it by instituting a program which did incorporate fair procedures. You don't go about it by making an accusation on page one or by calling some poor guy up and beating his brains out. You try to have a program that goes into the record and weeds out the security risks through a fair process. After all, Attorney General Brownell designed the program. Brownell had no use whatsoever for McCarthy and was dedicated to civil liberties and civil rights. Eisenhower enunciated exactly this kind of position, starting during the campaign, in Wisconsin.

QUESTION: He gave very sporadic attention to the preservation of civil liberties. The only thrust the public caught was: "We've got to get these traitors out of government." That was the emphasis of the program, and I'm saying that a different emphasis could have created different consensus sooner.

MR. EWALD: You say he could have speeded up the time table. Perhaps you're right. I would deny, however, that he made no attempt to enunciate these things because he did.

Do you think you could read the Dartmouth speech without knowing what Eisenhower thought?

QUESTION: No, but who was reading the Dartmouth speech? We are talking about the average man there who sees him waffle and apparently cancel it out in his next news conference. We don't want to go back and read the Dartmouth speech. That's already old hat.

MR. EWALD: I've given you Dartmouth. I'll give you Eisenhower's message to the American Library Association. I've given you the message to the three ecumenical leaders against J. B. Mathews. I'll give you the Boston speech. I'll give you the speech to the Anti-Defamation League of B'nai B'rith, and I've given you the press conference on the disappearance of the Communists-in-government issue. That's within a period of six months. What else? A security program set out to deal with the problem and restore the belief of the American people in the integrity of government. All of those things went on in 1953. Now if you say that he should have made twelve declarations instead of six, maybe he should. If you say that he should have speeded up the timetable, maybe he should. But the Eisenhower timetable as it worked through a year and a half did in fact instill that kind of consensus. And I cite Tony Lewis' having said that that's exactly what Ike did do.

Now if you say faster, faster, faster, faster, like the White Queen, I would agree. Everyone would have liked McCarthy dumped overboard sooner. Maybe he could have done it faster. But no one knows, and I tend to doubt it.

QUESTION: I'll give you three instances of strong Eisenhower oppositions to McCarthy: the Bohlen nomination, the firing of Mathews, and defending the CIA when McCarthy went after William Bundy. There were the three times when it is quite clear that Eisenhower did stand up to McCarthy. The speeches I don't see as of major significance. Against them you've got the instance of the Greek ship owners and McCarthy's forcing Stassen to back down—clearly a victory for McCarthy. You've got the instance of the Voice of America, which was seriously disrupted by pro-McCarthy forces.

And there was the firing of John Paton Davies, which was extremely distressing to the press because Davies had a lot of friends in the press.

MR. EWALD: That didn't happen until after McCarthy had been brought down. John Paton Davies was not dismissed until November 1954, one month before McCarthy's censure, five months after the end of the hearings.

QUESTION: Was it that late?

MR. EWALD: Yes. And because Dulles didn't fire him, McCarthy raised hell with Dulles.

QUESTION: I thought Davies was fired earlier. But you said one thing that puzzled me. You said the China hands in the State Department were fired under Truman. Who fired John Stewart Service?

MR. EWALD: John Stewart Service was fired under Acheson. O. Edmund Clubb was moved to another job and then quit. That's two. John Carter Vincent was on the ragged edge as Eisenhower came in. They didn't know what to do with him. Dulles let him retire with a pension, and McCarthy said he should have kicked him out and taken his pension away. The timetable you can argue with. But on the whole, Ike did pretty well. And I think the kind of consensus that you are asking for is the kind he would have agreed with. It exemplifies, I believe, what he was trying to do.